If you have a home computer with internet access you may:
-request an item be placed on hold
-renew an item that is overdue
-view titles and due dates checked out on your card
-view your own outstanding fines

To view your patron record from your home computer:
Click on the NSPL homepage:
http://nspl.suffolk.lib.ny.us

North Shore Public Library

GEORGE
ELIOT

COMPREHENSIVE RESEARCH
AND STUDY GUIDE

BLOOM'S
MAJOR
NOVELISTS

EDITED AND WITH AN
INTRODUCTION BY HAROLD BLOOM

CURRENTLY AVAILABLE

BLOOM'S MAJOR NOVELISTS

Jane Austen
The Brontës
Willa Cather
Stephen Crane
Don DeLillo
Charles Dickens
Fyodor Dostoevsky
George Eliot
William Faulkner
F. Scott Fitzgerald
Thomas Hardy
Nathaniel Hawthorne
Ernest Hemingway
Henry James
James Joyce
Franz Kafka
D. H. Lawrence
Herman Melville
Toni Morrison
Marcel Proust
Thomas Pynchon
John Steinbeck
Stendhal
Leo Tolstoy
Mark Twain
Alice Walker
Edith Wharton
Virginia Woolf

GEORGE
ELIOT

COMPREHENSIVE RESEARCH
AND STUDY GUIDE

BLOOM'S

MAJOR

NOVELISTS

EDITED AND WITH AN INTRODUCTION
BY HAROLD BLOOM

CHELSEA HOUSE
PUBLISHERS
A Haights Cross Communications Company
Philadelphia

First Printing
1 3 5 7 9 8 6 4 2

Library of Congress Cataloging-in-Publication Data
George Eliot / edited and with an introduction by Harold Bloom.
    p. cm. —(Bloom's major novelists)
Includes bibliographical references and index.
    ISBN 0-7910-7026-3
    1. Eliot, George, 1819–1880—Criticism and interpretation. 2. Women
and literature—England—History—19th century. I. Bloom, Harold. II.
Series.
    PR4688 .G37 2002
    823'.8—dc21

                                                        2002153025

Chelsea House Publishers
1974 Sproul Road, Suite 400
Broomall, PA 19008-0914

http://www.chelseahouse.com

Contributing Editor: Sarah Robbins

Cover design by Terry Mallon

Layout by EJB Publishing Services

CONTENTS

USER'S GUIDE

This volume is designed to present biographical, critical, and bibliographical information on the author and the author's best-known or most important works. Following Harold Bloom's editor's note and introduction is a concise biography of the author that discusses major life events and important literary accomplishments. A critical analysis of each novel follows, tracing significant themes, patterns, and motifs in the work. An annotated list of characters supplies brief information on the main characters in each work.

A selection of critical extracts, derived from previously published material, follows each thematic analysis. In most cases, these extracts represent the best analysis available from a number of leading critics. Because these extracts are derived from previously published material, they will include the original notations and references when available. Each extract is cited, and readers are encouraged to use the original publications as they continue their research. A bibliography of the author's writings, a list of additional books and articles on the author and their work, and an index of themes and ideas conclude the volume.

As with any study guide, this volume is designed as a supplement to the works being discussed, and is in no way intended as a replacement for those works. The reader is advised to read the text prior to using this study guide, and to keep it accessible for quick reference.

ABOUT THE EDITOR

Harold Bloom is Sterling Professor of the Humanities at Yale University and Henry W. and Albert A. Berg Professor of English at the New York University Graduate School. He is the author of over 20 books, and the editor of more than 30 anthologies of literary criticism.

Professor Bloom's works include *Shelley's Mythmaking* (1959), *The Visionary Company* (1961), *Blake's Apocalypse* (1963), *Yeats* (1970), *A Map of Misreading* (1975), *Kabbalah and Criticism* (1975), *Agon: Toward a Theory of Revisionism* (1982), *The American Religion* (1992), *The Western Canon* (1994), and *Omens of Millennium: The Gnosis of Angels, Dreams, and Resurrection* (1996). *The Anxiety of Influence* (1973) sets forth Professor Bloom's provocative theory of the literary relationships between the great writers and their predecessors. His most recent books include *Shakespeare: The Invention of the Human*, a 1998 National Book Award finalist, *How to Read and Why* (2000), and *Genius: A Mosiac of One Hundred Exemplary Creative Minds* (2002).

Professor Bloom earned his Ph.D. from Yale University in 1955 and has served on the Yale faculty since then. He is a 1985 MacArthur Foundation Award recipient and served as the Charles Eliot Norton Professor of Poetry at Harvard University in 1987–88. In 1999 he was awarded the prestigious American Academy of Arts and Letters Gold Medal for Criticism. Professor Bloom is the editor of several other Chelsea House series in literary criticism, including BLOOM'S MAJOR SHORT STORY WRITERS, BLOOM'S MAJOR NOVELISTS, BLOOM'S MAJOR DRAMATISTS, BLOOM'S MODERN CRITICAL INTERPRETATIONS, BLOOM'S MODERN CRITICAL VIEWS, and BLOOM'S BIOCRITIQUES.

EDITOR'S NOTE

My Introduction centers upon the crucial question of George Eliot's moral authority, which she converts into one of her principal aesthetic strengths.

So rich is the quality of the "Critical Views" that I choose among them with some diffidence.

The Mill on the Floss is particularly illuminated by Virginia Woolf and by three subsequent critics in her tradition: Gillian Beer, Elaine Showalter, and Mary Jacobus.

On *Silas Marner*, I am most deeply enlightened by Alexander Welsh.

Middlemarch, George Eliot's masterwork, seems to me to benefit most here by the perspectives of D.A. Miller and George Levine.

The problematic *Daniel Deronda* is studied incisively by Martin Price in its crucial first scene.

Harold Bloom

What can we mean when we speak of the "moral authority" of a great novelist? To invoke the phrase, in English, is to intimate George Eliot, rather than Charles Dickens, Henry James, or Joseph Conrad. This is hardly to deny *Bleak House*, *The Bostonians*, or *The Secret Agent* their wealth of moral insight, but rather recognizes an uniqueness in George Eliot.

That there is something grave and majestic that informs *Middlemarch*, we scarcely can evade sensing. The protagonist, Dorothea Brooke, is more than a secular St. Theresa; she is a preternaturally strong soul capable of fighting through her own errors. The strong figures who go under—Bulstrode, the peculiar Casaubon, the self-ruined Lydgate (precursor of Dick Diver in Scott Fitzgerald's *Tender is the Night*)—yield to flaws in their natures. Dorothea, like George Eliot, is a Wordsworthian. Projected sublimity, traditional heroism, is set aside, and a new sublimity shared by the self and nature takes its place.

Dorothea, in her moral intensity, is the ancestress of figures in Thomas Hardy and D.H. Lawrence, but her curious, inward strength has few analogues in other heroines. Henry James, subtly unnerved by *Middlemarch*, indulged in defensive fault-finding, much as he had done with *The Scarlet Letter*. What made James uncomfortable was a sublimity that his great characters, Isabel Archer in particular, were too evasive to sustain.

It has been too easy to confuse George Eliot's moral vision, as even Nietzsche showed, when he scorned her for supposedly believing that you could retain Christian morality while discarding the Christian God. George Eliot's advocacy of renunciation is not Christian, any more than Goethe's was. The moral sublime in Eliot is allied to Goethe's view that our virtues become our errors as we seek to expand life. Goethe, keenly ironical, is very different from George Eliot, who rarely allows herself irony. But then, no critic gets anywhere by bringing an ironic perspective to George Eliot.

Wisdom literature, in modern times, is very rare: who except George Eliot could write it? She surprises us by her affinities to the greatest poets—Shakespeare and Dante—affinities that are manifest in the dark individuality with which she endows the tragic Lydgate and the undefeated quester, Dorothea.

Moral authority in imaginative literature cannot be distinguished from clarity and power of intellect, and from the faculty of inventiveness. I cannot think of any novelist except for George Eliot who can be compared to Shakespeare and to Dante in these matters.

George Eliot

"The world was, first and foremost, for George Eliot, the moral, the intellectual world," wrote Henry James in 1885. In her work, the woman once called the greatest living writer of English fiction illuminated the common lives of her characters with the light of her extraordinary perception. In her life, she underwent countless evolutions. She was born Mary Anne Evans on November 22, 1819 at Arbury Park in Warwickshire. Her father, Robert Evans, the son of a Derbyshire carpenter who became overseer of the Arbury estate, was a staunch Tory and a member of the Church of England. The youngest of five children, Mary Anne was most devoted to her brother Issac. When her mother—Christiana Pearson, Evans' second wife—died in 1836 and her sister Chrissy married in 1837, the only female left in at home—and by default the housekeeper—changed her name to Mary Ann. At fifteen, she underwent a spiritual conversion to Evangelicalism and became devoted to Calvin's Doctrine of the Elect, predestination, and determinism. Her maternal aunt, a Methodist, instilled in her a belief in good works.

After Issac married, Mary Ann and her ailing father moved to Coventry in 1841. There, she was introduced to the Bray and Hennell families, whose intellectualism and reexamination of biblical studies called Mary Ann's religious convictions into question and prompted her to stop attending church with her father. However, this action so profoundly upset Robert Evans, who believed that a daughter owed obedience above all, that Mary Ann relented. Still, her associations allowed her an opportunity to translate from the German David Friedrich Strauss's *Das Leben Jesu* (*Life of Jesus*)—an effort to take the miraculous interpretation of Jesus's deeds and place them in an evolutionary setting—which was published in 1846.

Robert Evans died in 1849, and Mary Ann's small inheritance and freedom from responsibility took her first to Geneva and then to London, where she boarded with John Chapman, the editor of the *Westminster Review*. She soon began editing the "Belles Lettres" section of the magazine. While in London, she befriended many leading intellectuals, including Herbert Spencer and Harriet Martineau, grew more interested in the Positivist philosophy of August Comte, and changed her name again, to Marian. In 1852, she met George Henry Lewes—a writer and editor who was married, though distanced from his wife—and in 1853, she began a translation of Ludwig Feuerbach's *The Essence of Christianity*, a humanistic approach to Christianity stressing duty and discipline. It is the only book she published under her real name. When Marian consented to live with Lewes, first in Germany and then in London, she earned the disdain of her family, friends, and several of her colleagues. Though they were devoted to one another for the remainder of their lives, the couple never married.

In 1856, encouraged by Lewes and daunted by a lack of work and inspiration, Marian began her first work of fiction. The result, "Amos Barton," published in *Blackwood's Edinburgh Magazine* in 1857, was the first in the *Scenes from Clerical Life* trilogy, published in book form in 1858. From the very first, her fiction was published under the pseudonym George Eliot— "George" because of Lewes, and "Eliot" because, according to Marian, it was a "good, mouth-filling, easily pronounced word." Upon publication, Dickens wrote to this mysterious Eliot with praise, saying that if *Scenes* had not been written by a woman, then "should I believe I am a woman myself."

Eliot's first novel, *Adam Bede*, conceived as another clerical scene and based on her maternal aunt's story of an infant murder, was published in early 1859, placing her in the highest rank of Victorian novelists. It was followed the same year by the short story "The Lifted Veil," one of Eliot's only first-person narratives. *The Mill on the Floss*, a *Bildungsroman* based on memories of her childhood and largely on her relationship with her brother Issac, was published in 1860, in time for a spring trip to Italy, which would provide inspiration for future novels. In August she published the short story "Brother Jacob," about a man who pacifies his idiot brother, steals money from his mother's hoard, and runs off to the Indies only to be exposed as a fraud. It is unique to Eliot's work because it is her only story that does not portray a single character in a sympathetic light.

By late fall, Eliot and Lewes had made a decision not to have any children and were taking steps toward amassing a fortune;

Eliot began *Silas Marner*, and its publication in 1861 marked a change for the writer. For the first time, her childhood memories were not the dominant force—she employed more explicitly relations of ethics, aesthetics, and philosophy. Next came *Romola*, a historical novel set in Florence during Savonarola's career, published in 1862. Though the setting was far away from Eliot, the subject matter—the story of an independent-minded woman struggling against the conventions of society—was familiar to her work. Her next novel, *Felix Holt, the Radical*, depicted a rebellious son's rejection of his past and his struggle toward social reform. It was published in 1866, followed in 1868 by *The Spanish Gypsy*, a volume of dramatic verse.

By August of 1868, Eliot had begun recording information and ideas for *Middlemarch*, which was conceived as a portrait of societal circles familiar in her youth and a "study of provincial life." At first she saw the stories of Dr. Lydgate and Dorothea Brooke as independent—she joined them early 1871, and Book I appeared in December of that year. Seven parts followed in serial, and the entire novel was published in 1872 to the highest acclaim. Eliot's increasing involvement in society and her friendship with Emanuel Deutsch, whose work explored the parallels between Talmudic thought and the New Testament, provided fodder for her "international novel," which reached sketch stage in 1874 and appeared as *Daniel Deronda* in 1876. While Eliot was writing it, she also brought together a collection of poems published as *The Legend of Jubal, and Other Poems*. That volume was inscribed to an increasingly frail Lewes, who "has alone made my work possible for me."

Upon *Deronda's* publication, Eliot and Lewes embarked on a trip to Europe, bought a house in Surrey near Alfred Tennyson and his family, and learned tennis under the tutelage of John Cross, a young admirer introduced to the couple by Herbert Spencer in 1869. When Lewes died on November 30, 1878, Eliot never recovered from the blow. She published her last book, a collection of essays called *The Impressions of Theophrastus Such*, in 1879, and spent most of her time with Cross, a companion in grief (his mother had died a week after Lewes). The couple married in May 1880, made a brief tour of Italy, and settled into a new house, but Eliot died of kidney failure that same year, on December 22.

PLOT SUMMARY OF

The Mill on the Floss

The Mill on the Floss, which appeared in 1860, is a *Bildungsroman*—character building—novel that draws on George Eliot's childhood memories of rural England and addresses the challenge of satisfying both heart and mind under the constraints of an oppressive society. The actions and decisions of its characters illustrate the complications that arise from family ties and the strong impact of progress on provincial life. Maggie Tulliver's conflict between her own desires and her sense of duty leave her bereft of clarity; the very river that she and her brother Tom fight so hard to keep in their sights causes their eventual demise.

Maggie's tall stature, dark complexion, and penchant for troublemaking exasperate her superficial, fussy mother—formerly a Miss Dodson—and tickle her father, the proprietor of a mill that has been in his family for generations. When the story opens, the Tullivers are debating the education of Maggie's elder brother Tom, who, though equally headstrong, is less intelligent and ambitious than his sister. Mr. Tulliver means to send Tom to a parson, Mr. Stelling, to receive a gentleman's education so that he will not be forced into the family trade. When the Dodson sisters and their families convene for Easter breakfast, they are shocked that Mr. Tulliver wishes to educate Tom above his station; an ensuing argument prompts Mrs. Glegg, the eldest sister and leader, to storm out. Mr. Tulliver vows to repay Mrs. Glegg's £500 loan, but out of allegiance, refuses to collect on a loan that he made to his sister, Mrs. Moss.

Tom leaves to study with Mr. Stelling, an ambitious, if uninspired clergyman. Maggie visits and shows an interest in the subjects Tom abhors; though Stelling takes a liking to her, he insists women are incapable of intellectual pursuits. When Tom returns to St. Ogg's for the holidays, his father is distressed by an impending lawsuit against his nemesis, Mr. Wakem, over the use of the Floss River. When Tom returns to school in January, he meets his new schoolmate Philip Wakem, Wakem's humpbacked son. Despite their differences and the hostility brewing between their fathers, the boys find common ground; when Philip meets Maggie, he is impressed by the fiery, intelligent little girl.

Maggie, who by thirteen has begun to attend a boarding school with her cousin Lucy, is suddenly called home because her father has lost the lawsuit, and Wakem, who has a mortgage on the land, means to take over the mill. Tom returns as well; the children find their father rendered both bankrupt and ill and their mother lamenting over the imminent sale of her worldly possessions. The next morning, the Dodsons appear to discuss the plight of the Tullivers. Mrs. Moss visits as well, and when the Dodsons urge her to repay what she owes, Tom speaks up and insists his father wouldn't approve of the demand. When asked, Mr. Tulliver insists the note be destroyed and makes Tom vow to exact revenge on the Wakems. A few days later, against the advice of her sisters' husbands, Mrs. Tulliver visits Wakem and begs him not to buy the mill. Incensed by the inference that her husband speaks ill of him in public, Wakem goes through with the purchase and mortifies Mr. Tulliver by hiring him as the mill's manager.

The regret and humiliation of their parents is difficult for both children to handle. When Bob Jakin, a childhood friend of Tom's, gives Maggie *The Imitation of Christ* by Thomas à Kempis, the book inspires her to adopt a life of duty and selflessness. Though she attempts to sway her father, he is set on exacting revenge on Wakem. One day Maggie runs into Philip on a walk through her childhood haunt, the Red Deeps. Maggie insists that though her father's will keeps her away, she will never forget him. Philip gives her a book and vows to see her again. During the next year they meet in secret, and finally, Philip confesses his love for her.

Meanwhile, Tom is toiling to repay his father's debts. With the help of Mr. and Mrs. Glegg's "nest egg," he invests in a business venture with Bob Jakin that returns handsomely. Jakin tells Tom that he's seen Philip around the Red Deeps, and a tea-time visit with Mrs. Tulliver's sister Mrs. Pullet confirms the suspicion. Tom confronts Maggie, who confesses, and he makes her swear never again to speak to Philip. Together they meet Philip in the Red Deeps and Tom confronts him, accusing him of trifling with the family name. Soon after, Tom reveals his accumulation of wealth to his ecstatic parents. On the way back from the official repayment of his debts, Mr. Tulliver, a bit drunk, encounters Wakem and attacks him. He again falls ill and the next day, after making Tom swear he'll regain possession of the mill, he dies.

Several years later, Maggie, who's been working as a teacher, visits her cousin Lucy and her mother in St. Ogg's. When Mr. Stephen Guest, the son of Maggie's uncle's employer and Lucy's suitor, meets Maggie, he is smitten by her beauty and intelligence. When Maggie discovers that Philip is a good friend of Stephen's, she tells Lucy what has passed between them. Maggie asks Tom to absolve her of her promise against Philip. He unfeelingly agrees, accusing her of purposely committing wrongdoing. Maggie tells her brother she's given up the notion of taking Philip as a lover, but when Philip and Maggie rekindle their friendship, Maggie confides to Lucy that she'd marry Philip, if only her father wouldn't object. Lucy realizes that Tom means to regain possession of the mill and asks Philip to speak to his father on behalf of the Tullivers. Philip reveals his love for Maggie to his father, who at first strongly objects, but later softens. He agrees to give up the mill as long as he doesn't have to associate with Tom.

During the next few days Maggie and Stephen become more attached to one another; Maggie, resolute, plans to leave St. Ogg's for another teaching position. When Stephen kisses her at a dance, she recoils. Several days later, he comes to visit her at her Aunt Moss's house and confesses his love. Maggie objects, saying she means to marry no one else but Philip. Sick with worry and jealousy, Philip cancels a planned boat ride with Lucy and Maggie and sends Stephen instead. But Lucy is also absent, which leaves Stephen and Maggie alone. Stephen rows Maggie past their planned meeting point and proposes marriage to her. The weather changes, leaving them adrift dangerously far from home. Holding hands, the two board a larger ship bound for Mudport, and finally, Maggie tells Stephen they shall not return together.

Maggie returns to scorn and disapproval—Tom will not take her into their childhood home, so she boards with Bob Jakin. She begins visiting the clergyman Dr. Kenn, who expresses sympathy for her plight. Soon, however, rumors of an affair between

Maggie and Dr. Kenn terminate their relations. Lucy, who has been ill with despair, visits, and a letter from Philip brings forgiving words, as well. The weather becomes violently rainy, and a few days into the storm, Maggie receives a letter from Stephen, begging her to come to him. Though she feels a strange temptation, she resolves to bear the pain she has caused others until her death. Just then, water from the Floss River rushes under Bob Jakin's door. Maggie wakes the family, takes one of their boats to Dorlcote Mill, and rescues Tom. They set off to retrieve Lucy, but before they arrive, the boat capsizes and Maggie and Tom, hands clasped, drown together. Years later, Philip, Stephen, and Lucy together, visit their graves.

The Mill on the Floss

The protagonist of the story, **Maggie Tulliver** is a mischievous child who grows into a strong-willed, intelligent, and striking woman. She struggles with her sense of duty to her family and her desire to follow her passions.

Tom Tulliver, Maggie's brother, has the Dodson complexion and therefore is the favored child. He is as hardworking and determined as Maggie, though not as intelligent. He has no interest in intellectual pursuits but succeeds at making money in order to deliver his family from debt. His allegiance to his father's wish that he punish the Wakems eventually estranges him from his younger sister.

Elizabeth Tulliver, formerly a Miss Dodson, is Maggie and Tom's mother and Mr. Tulliver's wife. She is shallow and somewhat preoccupied with material possessions. When her husband loses the mill and his money, she's most worried about her dishes and silver. She favors Tom and is often irritated by Maggie's willfulness.

Edward Tulliver is a kindhearted man who has had Dorlcorte Mill in his family for generations. He wishes the best for Tom, but dotes on Maggie; though he disapproves of his sister's marriage to Mr. Moss, he supports her because he hopes Tom would do the same. When he loses the mill, he becomes ill and vengeful.

A cousin of Tom and Maggie's, **Lucy Deane** reintroduces Maggie to Phillip Wakem at the end of the novel. As a child, her blond curls and sweet demeanor make her the subject of envy among the Dodson sisters. As an adult, she is courted by Stephen Guest and is anxious to reunite Maggie and Philip Wakem.

Philip Wakem is the hunchbacked son of Lawyer Wakem who finds solace from his affliction in music, art, and his studies. He is a schoolmate of Tom's at Mr. Stelling's school and falls in love with Maggie when they meet again after her father goes bankrupt.

Lawyer Wakem is a powerful member of the St. Ogg's community who has contempt for Mr. Tulliver.

Stephen Guest, the son of a rich family, courts Lucy Deane but ends up falling in love with Maggie Tulliver instead.

Formerly Miss Jane Dodson, **Mrs. Glegg** is the leader of the four Dodson sisters. She's miserly, domineering, and often disapproving, but stands by Maggie at the end of the novel. **Mr. Glegg** is a retired wool-stapler and a frugal, good-natured man.

Formerly Miss Susan Dodson, **Mrs. Deane** is the quietest of the sisters—she dies before the end of the novel. **Mr. Deane** is a self-made city man who typifies the new ways of St. Ogg's and works for Guest and Company.

Formerly Miss Sophy Dodson, **Mrs. Pullet** is the closest sister to Mrs. Tulliver. They share a love of household goods. **Mr. Pullet** is overworked and doesn't say much.

Luke Moggs is the miller of the Mill on the Floss, and a faithful employee of Mr. Tulliver.

Rev. Walter Stelling is the tutor of Tom and Phillip Wakem. He uses his work as a means to an end and wants to rise in the world. Despite his ambition and large presence, he lacks imagination and openmindedness.

The minister of St. Ogg's, **Dr. Kenn** takes Maggie into confidence.

Mr. Tulliver's sister Margaret, or "Aunt Gritty," **Mrs. Moss** is also Maggie's godmother. She is patient and loving, and the mother of eight children. Mr. Tulliver disapproved of the marriage because **Mr. Moss** doesn't have much character—in order to support his family, he has become a "machine horse."

CRITICAL VIEWS ON
The Mill on the Floss

VIRGINIA WOOLF ON MAGGIE TULLIVER AND ELIOT'S CREATION OF A HEROINE

[Virginia Woolf, a major British novelist, essayist, and critic, was one of the leaders of modernism, incorporating stream-of-consciousness into her fiction writing. She's most famous for novels *Mrs. Dalloway* (1925), *To The Lighthouse* (1927), and *The Waves* (1931), and for the feminist treatise *A Room of One's Own* (1929). Here she discusses the demands of complex heroines such as Maggie Tulliver.]

Those who fall foul of George Eliot do so, we incline to think, on account of her heroines; and with good reason; for there is no doubt that they bring out the worst of her, lead her into difficult places, make her self-conscious, didactic, and occasionally vulgar. Yet if you could delete the whole sisterhood you would leave a much smaller and a much inferior world, albeit a world of greater artistic perfection and far superior jollity and comfort. In accounting for her failure in so far as it was a failure, one recollects that she never wrote a story until she was thirty-seven, and that by the time she was thirty-seven she had come to think of herself with a mixture of pain and something like resentment. For long she preferred not to think of herself at all. Then, when the first flush of creative energy was exhausted and self-confidence had come to her, she wrote more and more from the personal standpoint, but she did so without the unhesitating abandonment of the young. Her self-consciousness is always marked when her heroines say what she herself would have said. She disguised them in every possible way. She granted them beauty and wealth into the bargain; she invented, more improbably, a taste for brandy. But the disconcerting and stimulating fact remained that she was compelled by the very power of her genius to step forth in person upon the quiet bucolic scene.

The noble and beautiful girl who insisted upon being born

into the Mill on the Floss is the most obvious example of the ruin which a heroine can strew about her. Humour controls her and keeps her lovable so long as she is small and can be satisfied by eloping with the gipsies or hammering nails into her doll; but she develops; and before George Eliot knows what has happened she has a full-grown woman on her hands demanding what neither gipsies, nor dolls, nor St. Ogg's itself is capable of giving her. First Philip Wakem is produced, and later Stephen Guest. The weakness of the one and the coarseness of the other have often been pointed out; but both, in their weakness and coarseness, illustrate not so much George Eliot's inability to draw the portrait of a man, as the uncertainty, the infirmity, and the fumbling which shook her hand when she had to conceive a fit mate for a heroine. She is in the first place driven beyond the home world she knew and loved, and forced to set foot in middle-class drawing-rooms where young men sing all the summer morning and young women sit embroidering smoking-caps for bazaars. She feels herself out of her element, as her clumsy satire of what she calls "good society" proves.

> Good society has its claret and its velvet carpets, its dinner engagements six weeks deep, its opera, and its faëry ball rooms ... gets its science done by Faraday and its religion by the superior clergy who are to be met in the best houses; how should it have need of belief and emphasis?

There is no trace of humour or insight there, but only the vindictiveness of a grudge which we feel to be personal in its origin. But terrible as the complexity of our social system is in its demands upon the sympathy and discernment of a novelist straying across the boundaries, Maggie Tulliver did worse than drag George Eliot from her natural surroundings. She insisted upon the introduction of the great emotional scene. She must love; she must despair; she must be drowned clasping her brother in her arms. The more one examines the great emotional scenes the more nervously one anticipates the brewing and gathering and thickening of the cloud which will burst upon our heads at the moment of crisis in a shower of disillusionment and verbosity. It is partly that her hold upon dialogue, when it is not dialect, is slack; and partly that she seems to shrink with an elderly dread of fatigue from the effort of emotional concentration. She allows her heroines to talk too much. She has little verbal felicity. She lacks the unerring taste which chooses one sentence and compresses the heart of the scene within that. "Whom are you going to dance with?" asked Mr. Knightley, at the Westons' ball. "With you, if you will ask me," said Emma; and she has said enough. Mrs. Casaubon would have talked for an hour and we should have looked out of the window.

Yet, dismiss the heroines without sympathy, confine George Eliot to the agricultural world of her "remotest past," and you not only diminish her greatness but lose her true flavour. That greatness is here we can have no doubt. The width of the prospect, the large strong outlines of the principal features, the ruddy light of the early books, the searching power and reflective richness of the later tempt us to linger and expatiate beyond our limits. But it is upon the heroines that we would cast a final glance.

—Virginia Woolf, "George Eliot." *Discussions of George Eliot*, ed. Richard Stang, (Boston: D.C. Heath and Company, 1960): 28–29.

GILLIAN BEER ON PASSION AS INTELLECTUAL NEED

[Gillian Beer is the King Edward VII Professor of English Literature and an Honorary Fellow at Girton College, Cambridge University. She is also the author of *Meredith: A Change of Masks*, *Darwin's Plots*, and *Forging the Missing Link*. Here she discusses Maggie's learning as a kind of witchcraft and the contrast, in the fantasies and fairy tales she encounters, between darkness and light.]

In Maggie, passion takes the form of vehement intellectual need experienced as emotion. Desire for knowledge, for 'more instruments playing together', had traditionally been enregistered as the man's story. Faust and his wild passion for full possession of the world that knowledge may open, is saved by the innocent, stay-at-home, untutored Gretchen. Steadfast love is divided from the thirst for knowledge, polarised as female and male. George Eliot rejects that polarisation, first in Maggie, and then, more and more powerfully in the later novels by means of the polymathic narrative which, through learning, constantly discovers emotional connection. The writing ranges freely through and beyond such oppositions, but it also experiences them. (...)

> 'Oh I'll tell you what that means. It's a dreadful picture, isn't it? But I can't help looking at it. That old woman in the water's a witch—they've put her in to find out whether she's a witch or no, and if she swims she's a witch, if she's drowned—and killed, you know—she's innocent, and not a witch, but only a poor silly old woman. But what good would it do her then, you know, when she was drowned? Only, I suppose, she'd go to heaven, and God would make it up to her.' (*The Mill*, I, p. 21, Bk. I, ch. 3)

Maggie here cites the tale of the witch in Defoe's *History of the Devil*. The witch epitomises Maggie's bind. If she is innocent, she drowns. If she bobs up again, she is guilty. Is Maggie's drowning used in some half-magical way to prove her innocence? If so, such innocence is useless. Like the witch, Maggie is dead. Only the narrator can 'make it up to her'. The last chapter, indeed, is entitled 'The Final Rescue', and that rescue is undertaken by the writer. Within the work, Maggie herself makes jokes about another such magical ordering in novels and fairy-tales, that of the blond and the dark heroine. The blond represents restraint and social order, the dark, passion and disruption. The blond is bound to win, and Maggie resents that. So do we. Lucy sees Maggie's learning as 'witchcraft': 'part of your general uncanniness' (II, p. 187, Bk. VI, ch. 3).

> 'I didn't finish the book,' said Maggie. 'As soon as I came to the blond-haired young lady reading in the park, I shut it up, and determined to read no further. I foresaw that that light-complexioned girl would win away all the love from Corinne and make her miserable. I'm determined to read no more books where the blond-haired women carry away all the happiness. I should begin to have a prejudice against them. If you could give me some story, now, where the dark woman tri-

umphs, it would restore the balance. I want to avenge Rebecca and Flora MacIvor, and Minna and all the rest of the dark unhappy ones.' (II, p. 102, Bk. V, Ch. 4)

The work playfully draws attention to its own order and knowingly prognosticates what comes to seem inevitable: Maggie's defeat. Yet it presages, too, the paradoxical sense of Maggie's triumph and vengeance with which, despite her death, the book concludes.

The novel is full of meaning glimpsed from earlier literature. Maggie is determinedly shut out by the education system, with its stereotypes of male and female, from classical learning, though she demonstrates her readiness and skill at Mr Stelling's house (Jacobus, 1981, pp. 207–22). But the magical fragmentariness also feeds her:

She presently made up her mind to skip the rules in the Syntax—the examples became so absorbing. The mysterious sentences, snatched from an unknown context,—like strange horns of beasts, and leaves of unknown plants, brought from some far-off region—gave boundless scope to her imagination, and were all the more fascinating because they were in a peculiar tongue of their own, which she could learn to interpret. (I, p. 228, Bk. II, ch. 1)

Both Tom and Maggie, for differing reasons, are dependent on Philip, the wounded Philoctetes, to give them access to the warmth of learning in their lives. The roused meaning of flat text needs a speaking voice to make it heard. Learning can enter their youth as story:

He listened with great interest to a new story of Philip's about a man who had a very bad wound in his foot, and cried out so dreadfully with the pain that his friends could bear with him no longer, but put him ashore on a desert island, with nothing but some wonderful poisoned arrows to kill animals with for food.
'I didn't roar out a bit, you know,' Tom said, 'and I daresay my foot was as bad as his. It's cowardly to roar.'

But Maggie would have it that when anything hurt you very much, it was quite permissible to cry out, and it was cruel of people not to bear it. She wanted to know if Philoctetes had a sister, and why she didn't go with him on the desert island and take care of him. (I, pp. 285–6, Bk. II, ch. 6)

These stories are shared complicitly by author and reader, weaving connections not always apparent to those within the text. Like metaphor, they allow meaning to emerge without settling. And yet George Eliot will not allow the reader to remain comfortable within the possession of these connections: 'light irony' and easy cultural pretensions may be bought dear, and Maggie's 'false quantities' go with a deeper learning than Tom's.

Now and then, that sort of enthusiasm finds a far-echoing voice that comes from an experience springing out of the deepest need. And it was by being brought within the long lingering vibrations of such a voice that Maggie, with her girl's face and unnoted sorrows, found an effort and a hope that helped her through years of loneliness, making out a faith for herself without the aid of established authorities and appointed guides—for they were not at hand, and her need was pressing. (II, p. 38, Bk. IV, ch. 3)

Thomas à Kempis's *Imitation of Christ* speaks to Maggie as voice, in away that is made to sustain the emphasis of the address to the reader immediately afterwards.

But good society, floated on gossamer wings of light irony, is of very expensive production; requiring nothing less than a wide and arduous national life condensed in unfragrant deafening factories, cramping itself in mines, sweating at furnaces, grinding, hammering, weaving under more or less oppression of carbonic acid—or else, spread over sheepwalks, and scattered in lonely houses and huts on the clayey or chalky cornlands, where the rainy days look dreary. This wide national life is based entirely on emphasis—the emphasis of want. (II, p. 37, Bk. IV, ch. 3)

Philip says of himself '"my voice is middling—like everything else in me".' But Philip is the interpreter, a redeemed version of Latimer, able despite his physical debility to see precisely and kindly into the sensibility of others. He is kind, in some ways more kind or 'kinned' to Maggie than her brother, though in the end it is blood-bond and primitive memory that hold her. His exclusion from active life sets him alongside Maggie in a way which confuses likeness and difference. He tempts Maggie with his offer to be 'brother and teacher', but he can never satisfy her sexually.

For Maggie, there can be no accommodation with society, because the community in which she has grown up, and the culture of which this is an expression, will accord her nature no recognition.

> 'Girls can't do Euclid: can they, sir?'
> 'They can pick up a little of everything, I daresay,' said Mr Stelling. 'They've a great deal of superficial cleverness; but they couldn't go far into anything. They're quick and shallow.'
> As for Maggie, she had hardly ever been so mortified. She had been so proud to be called 'quick' all her little life, and now it appeared that this quickness was the brand of inferiority. (I, pp. 232–3, Bk. II, ch. 1)

She is one of the aberrations of breeding:

> 'An' a pleasant sort o' soft woman may go on breeding you stu-pid lads and cute wenches, till it's like as if the world was turned topsy-turvy.' (I, p. 24, Bk. I, ch. 3)

She resists bonding herself to other women, because they represent so much she must gainsay.

> 'I think all women are crosser than men,' said Maggie. 'Aunt Glegg's a great deal crosser than Uncle Glegg, and mother scolds me more than father does.'
> 'Well, *you'll* be a woman some day,' said Tom, 'so you needn't talk.'
> 'But I shall be a *clever* woman,' said Maggie, with a toss.
> 'Oh, I daresay, and a nasty conceited thing. Everybody'll hate you.' (I, p. 226, Bk. II, ch. 1)

The work excels at taut humour which catches the sound of women gossiping, pinched into the forms of their narrow society. The aunts with cheerful gloom give voice to the domestic powers and repression of St Ogg's.

Maggie's other favourite childhood reading, *Pilgrim's Progress*, is a story of tribulations ending in triumph and delight. Loved as that model is, it is also eschewed, though something of its mood of triumphal reconcilement is retained. Like Christian, Maggie and Tom go down into the river. Through careful, humanistic negatives, George Eliot allows a secular faith in human accord to predict this final scene:

> there was an undefined sense of reconcilement with her broth-er: what quarrel, what harshness, what unbelief in each other can subsist in the presence of a great calamity, when all the artificial vesture of our life is gone, and we are all one with another in primitive mortal needs? (II, p. 395, Bk. VII, ch. 5)

The book refuses to consider the question: how long can that oneness survive after calamity?—unless Tom and Maggie's immediate death implies a dour answer.

—Gillian Beer, *George Eliot*, (Bloomington: Indiana University Press, 1986): 87–93.

ELAINE SHOWALTER ON SEXUAL IDENTITIES AND INSECURITIES

[Elaine Showalter is an initiator of feminist criticism in the United States. A former recipient of a Guggenheim fellowship and a Rockefeller Humanities fellowship, she is the author of *The Female Malady: Women, Madness, and English Culture* (1830-1980) and the editor of the textbook *Women's Liberation and Literature*. Here she explores Eliot's emphasis on feminine passion and male repression.]

Eliot's original title for the novel (she was calling it "Sister Maggie" until January 1860) and the title of the first book ("Boy and Girl") highlight the relationship of Maggie and Tom, and the conceptualization of feminine passion and masculine repression that are the extremes of sex-role conditioning. One Victorian critic, Richard Simpson, observed about Eliot that "the antithesis of passion and duty figures itself to her mind as a kind of sexual distinction; so that if woman could be defecated [*sic*] from all male fibres, she would be all passion, as man, purged of all feminine qualities, would be all hard duty." Tom Tulliver is an instance of a male nearly pure; the purest form of woman is "a being with black hair and large dark eyes ... a mass of yearnings, passions, and feelings,"[59] in short, Maggie.

Eliot goes to some pains to show how the differences in expectations, education, and daily treatment by the family form Maggie and Tom. Tom's life is not easy, any more than Maggie's is, but the disciplines to which he is called are lighter for him to assume because they are basically in accordance with his personality. The qualities that denote Tom's mind—will, self-control, self-righteousness, narrowness of imagination, and a disposition to dominate and to blame others, all the traits of the authoritarian personality—Eliot sees as masculine, and the correlatives of status and self-esteem. Tom is never so "susceptible," never so much "like a girl," as when he is made to feel stupid at school.[60] If there is any single aspect of sexual differentiation that Eliot points to as significant, it is this difference in self-esteem that depends upon the approbation of the family and social circle. Tom learns when very young not to doubt himself, while Maggie, to the end of her life, is self-doubting and unassertive. Maggie's self-esteem is pitifully dependent on Tom's love, and she will sacrifice any legitimate claim of her own personality to avoid rejection by him.[61]

Unlike Tom Tulliver, Stephen Guest, and Lucy Deane, Maggie Tulliver and Philip Wakem are insecure in their sexual identity, and this insecurity is one of the shared emotions that brings them together. Because he is a cripple, Philip has led a girl's life; he has been barred from sports and swordplay and ultimately forced to be "perfectly quiescent," as immobilized as Maggie herself. It is a commonplace in feminine fiction for the sensitive man to be represented as maimed; Linton Heathcliff in *Wuthering Heights*, Phineas Fletcher in Dinah Craik's *John*

Halifax, Gentleman, Charlie Edmondstone in Charlotte Yonge's *The Heir of Redclyffe,* and even such late versions as Colin Cravan in Frances Hodgson Burnett's *The Secret Garden* all suggest that men condemned to lifelong feminine roles display the personality traits of frustrated women. Philip, for example, has enough empathy to penetrate Maggie's mournful resignation, but he also has a "peevish susceptibility," compounded of "nervous irritation" and the "heart-bitterness produced by the sense of his deformity."[62]

Because he shares many of Maggie's dilemmas, Philip is uniquely qualified to analyze them for her and for the reader. Maggie is unable to channel her passionate energy into productive work, to yoke her pride, ambition, and intelligence into a single effective force, as Tom does, and she therefore must find some strategy for subduing her own nature and securing Tom's approval. Her tactics, as Philip perceives, are escapist and renunciatory. In most conflicts Maggie cannot face the truth about her own feelings and has to persuade herself that other people are making her do things. In her clandestine meetings with Philip in the Red Deeps, she is vaguely aware that he is sexually unattractive, and that she is becoming entrapped in an exploitative and oppressive relationship; but rather than admitting these feelings and accepting the responsibility of acting upon them, she allows the meetings to be discovered and passively accompanies Tom to a showdown with Philip. It is clear that Tom, although he is brutal and even sadistic, speaks truthfully to Philip, and that in accusing Philip of taking advantage of his sister's loneliness he is acting out some of Maggie's anger and aggression. At the end of the scene Maggie is "conscious of a certain dim background of relief in the forced separation from Philip,"[63] but she deceives herself into believing that she is simply relieved to be free of concealment. When Maggie *does* feel sexually attracted to a man, she has no vocabulary for her emotions and must define her physical excitement as "love"; she must pretend that Stephen Guest has kidnapped her and that she is helplessly drifting away, when it is obvious that they are colluding in the elopement. Even after her awakening in the boat, when she makes the decision to resist Stephen, Maggie cannot move toward a purposeful construction of her life.

59. "George Eliot's Novels," *Home and Foreign Review* III (1863), in *George Eliot: The Critical Heritage*, p. 239.

60 *Mill on the Floss*, p. 126. Blackwood wrote her that "Tom's life at Stelling's is perfect. It is perfectly wonderful how you have been able to realise the boy's feelings. Men will read it like reminiscences of what they themselves felt—suffered" (*George Eliot Letters*, iii, p. 263).

61. For an extremely interesting Horneyan analysis of Maggie's defensive strategies, see Bernard J. Paris, "The Inner Conflicts of Maggie Tulliver," *A Psychological Approach to Fiction*, Bloomington, 1974.

62. *Mill on the Floss*, II, ch. 4, p. 148.

63. Ibid., V, ch. 6, p. 305.

> —Elaine Showalter, *A Literature of Their Own: British Women Novelists from Bronte to Lessing*, (Princeton, New Jersey: Princeton University Press, 1977): 126–128.

MARY JACOBUS ON MAXIMS AND THE LANGUAGE THAT UNDOES THEM

[Mary Jacobus is Professor of English at the University of Cambridge. She is the author of *Romanticism, Writing, and Sexual Difference* and *Psychoanalysis & the Scene of Reading*. Here she discusses the role of language and rules and how the implication of maxims in Tom's education inspires Maggie's quest for knowledge.]

Eliot's account of Tom's schooling in "School-Time," the opening chapter of Book 2, provides just such a thematic treatment—a lesson in antifeminist pedagogy which goes beyond its immediate implications for women's education to raise more far-reaching questions about the functioning of both sexual ideology and language. Take Maggie's puzzlement at one of the many maxims found in the Eton Grammar, a required text for the unfortunate Tom. As often, rules and examples prove hard to tell apart:

> The astronomer who hated women generally caused [Maggie] so much puzzling speculation that she one day asked Mr. Stelling if all astronomers hated women, or whether it was

only this particular astronomer. But, forestalling his answer, she said,

"I suppose it's all astronomers: because you know, they live up in high towers, and if the women came there, they might talk and hinder them from looking at the stars."

Mr. Stelling liked her prattle immensely. (p. 220)

What we see here is a textbook example of the way in which individual misogyny becomes generalized—"maximized," as it were—in the form of a patriarchal put-down. Maggie may have trouble construing "*ad unam mulieres,*" or "all to a woman," but in essence she has got it right. Just to prove her point, Mr. Stelling (who himself prefers the talk of women to star gazing) likes her "prattle," a term used only of the talk of women and children. Reduced to his idea of her, Maggie can only mimic man's talk.

Inappropriate as he is in other respects for Tom's future career, Mr. Stelling thus proves an excellent schoolmaster to his latent misogyny. His classroom is also an important scene of instruction for Maggie, who learns not only that all astronomers to a man hate women in general but that girls can't learn Latin; that they are quick and shallow, mere imitators ("this small apparatus of shallow quickness," Eliot playfully repeats); and that everybody hates clever women, even if they are amused by the prattle of clever little girls (pp. 214, 221, 216). It's hard not to read with one eye on her creator. Maggie, it emerges, rather fancies herself as a linguist, and Eliot too seems wishfully to imply that she has what one might call a "gift" for languages—a gift, perhaps, for ambiguity too. Women, we learn, don't just talk, they double-talk, like language itself; that's just the trouble for boys like Tom:

"I know what Latin is very well," said Maggie, confidently. "Latin's a language. There are Latin words in the Dictionary. There's bonus, a gift."

"Now, you're just wrong there, Miss Maggie!" said Tom, secretly astonished. "You think you're very wise! But 'bonus' means 'good,' as it happens—bonus, bona, bonum."

"Well, that's no reason why it shouldn't mean 'gift,'" said Maggie stoutly. "It may mean several things. Almost every word does." (p. 214)

And if words may mean several things, general rules or maxims may prove less universal than they claim to be and lose their authority. Perhaps only "this particular astronomer" was a woman-hater or hated only one woman in particular. Special cases or particular contexts—"the special circumstances that mark the individual lot" (p. 628)—determine or render indeterminate not only judgment but meaning too. The rules of language itself make Tom's rote learning troublesome to him. How can he hope to construe his sister when her relation to language proves so treacherous—her difference so shifting a play of possibility, like the difference within language itself, destabilizing terms such as "wrong" and "good"?

Maggie, a little parody of her author's procedures in *The Mill on the Floss*, decides "to skip the rule in the syntax—the examples became so absorbing":

> These mysterious sentences snatched from an unknown con-
> text,—like strange horns of beasts and leaves of unknown
> plants, brought from some far-off region, gave boundless
> scope to her imagination, and were all the more fascinating
> because they were in a peculiar tongue of their own, which she
> could learn to interpret. It was really very interesting—the
> Latin Grammar that Tom had said no girls could learn: and
> she was proud because she found it interesting. The most frag-
> mentary examples were her favourites. Mors omnibus est com-
> munis would have been jejune, only she liked to know the
> Latin; but the fortunate gentleman whom every one congrat-
> ulated because he had a son "endowed with such a disposition"
> afforded her a great deal of pleasant conjecture, and she was
> quite lost in the "thick grove penetrable by no star," when Tom
> called out,
> "Now, then, Maggie, give us the Grammar!" (pp. 217–18)

Whereas maxims lace her up in formulas, "these mysterious sentences" give boundless scope to Maggie's imagination; for her, as for her author (who makes them foretell her story), they are whole fictional worlds, alternative realities, transformations of the familiar into the exotic and strange. In their foreignness she finds herself, until roused by Tom's peremptory call, as she is later to be recalled by his voice from the Red Deeps. Here, however, it is Maggie who teaches Tom his most important lesson, that the "dead" languages had once been living: "that there had once been people upon the earth who were so fortunate as to know Latin without learning it through the medium of the Eton Grammar" (p. 221). The idea—or, rather, fantasy—of a language that is innate rather than acquired, native rather than incomprehensibly foreign, is a consoling one for the unbookish miller's son; but it holds out hope for Maggie too, and presumably also for her creator. Though Latin stands in for cultural imperialism and for the outlines of a peculiarly masculine and elitist classical education from which women have traditionally been excluded, Maggie can learn to interpret it. The "peculiar tongue" had once been spoken by women, after all— and they had not needed to learn it from Mr. Stelling or the institutions he perpetuates. Who knows, she might even become an astronomer herself, or, like Eliot, a writer who by her pen name had refused the institutionalization of sexual difference as cultural exclusion. Tom and Mr. Stelling tell Maggie that "Girls never learn such things"; "They've a great deal of superficial cleverness but they couldn't go far into anything" (pp. 214, 221). But going far into things—and going far—is the author's prerogative in *The Mill on the Floss*. Though Maggie's quest for knowledge ends in death, as Virginia Woolf thought Eliot's own had ended, killing off this small apparatus of shallow quickness may have been the necessary sacrifice in order for Eliot herself to become an interpreter of the exotic possibilities contained in mysterious sentences. Maggie—unassimilable, incomprehensible, "fallen"—is her text, a "dead" language which thereby gives all the greater scope to authorial imaginings, making it possible for the writer to come into being.

—Mary Jacobus, *Reading Women, Essays in Feminist Criticism*, (Columbia University Press, 1986): 69–72.

W.D. HOWELLS ON THE FORCED TOUCH OF TRAGEDY

[W.D. Howells was a critic, novelist, and playwright as famous for his friendship with luminaries such as Mark Twain as he was for his exhaustive work. He wrote the travel book *Venetian Life*, and the novels *Indian Summer* and *A Hazard of New Fortunes*. His best-known work of criticism is *Criticism and Fiction*. Here he explains why Eliot's decision to end her novel in flood and tragedy seems heavy-handed.]

It is by her nature, complex, passionate, sensuous, by her sex, intellectualized and spiritualized, that Maggie Tulliver is most important to the reader. In her relations to her brother, which are apparently the chief interest of the book, she is interestingly and novelly studied; but these, though they involve the catastrophe, do not involve the climax. That is reached, as it seems to me, not when she and Tom are drowned together in the flood of the Floss, but when her reason and her conscience are provisionally overborne by her love for Stephen Guest, and she floats with him down a tide and out upon a sea more perilous than any inundation, and saves herself only by a powerful impulse of her will, which is almost a convulsion. The fruition of her love would have been a double treason, treason to her cousin Lucy, who was Guest's betrothed, and treason to Philip Wakem, to whom she was herself pledged; and the sense of this blackened it with guilt, and turned it to despair, even while she yielded and yielded to the love of being loved. Never has an unhappy passion been more faithfully studied in a character with strength enough finally to forbid it; or more subtly felt from that first moment when Maggie begins to rejoice in her beauty because of her love for the man who loves it, fill that last moment when she refuses to marry him, and goes back to suffer shame rather than to merit shame. Every step of the way is accurately and firmly traced up to that passage where Stephen Guest comes to ask her to row with him on the river, and from which there seems no retreat....

It does not seem to me that the true logic of the late is Maggie's death with Tom Tulliver, or Stephen's marriage with Lucy. It is a forced touch where the husband and wife stand together beside the grave of the brother and sister; but in the novels, the best of the novels, fifty years ago, they forced their touches rather more than they do now. To kill people or to marry them is to beg the question; but into some corner the novelist is commonly driven who deals with a problem. It is only life that can deal masterfully with problems, and life does not solve them by referring them to another life or by stifling them with happiness. How life would have solved the problem of Maggie Tulliver I am not quite prepared to say; but I have my revolt against George Eliot's solution. All the more I must own that the heroine's character, from the sort of undisciplined, imaginative, fascinating little girl we see her at first, into the impassioned, bewildered, self-disciplined woman we see her at last is masterly. Having given my opinion that her supreme expression is in her relation to her lover, I have my doubts, or at least my compunctions in behalf of her relation to her brother. Unquestionably the greatest pathos of the story appeals to us from her relation to her brother. The adoring dependence, the grieving indignation, the devotion, the revolt, the submission, and the reunion which make up her love for him is such a study of sisterly affection as I should not know where to match. The very conditions of her intellectual and emotional superiority involve a moral inferiority to the brute simplicity, the narrow integrity, the heroic truth of the more singly natured man. Maggie saw life more whole than Tom, but that part of it which he saw he discerned with a clearness denied to her large but cloudy vision. It is a great and beautiful story, which one reads with a helpless wonder that such a book should ever be in any wise superseded, or should not constantly keep the attention at least of those fitted to feel its deep and lasting significance.

—W.D. Howells, *The Mill on the Floss* by George Eliot, Vol. IX. *Harvard Classics Shelf of Fiction* (New York: P.F. Collier & Son, 1917; Bartleby.com, 2000).

JOAN BENNETT ON THE BREADTH OF ELIOT'S COMMUNITIES

[Joan Bennett is the author of *George Eliot: Her Mind and Art*. Here she discusses how the description of setting in *The Mill on the Floss* allows the reader to understand the adversity Maggie faces.]

In her own view the lack of symmetry in *The Mill on the Floss* was responsible for her imperfect fulfilment of her intention, and for the dissatisfaction that most readers feel about the end of that novel:

> ... the tragedy is not adequately prepared. This is a defect which I felt while writing the third volume, and have felt ever since the MS. left me. The *Epische Breite* into which I was beguiled by love of my subject in the first two volumes, caused a want of proportionate fullness in the treatment of the third, which I shall always regret.[2]

The regret is justified in so far as the compression of the Maggie and Stephen episode contributes to its faulty presentation. Yet the epic breadth of the first two volumes is warranted by the completeness with which we come to understand the pressure of her surroundings on Maggie's developing personality which will, in turn, condition the central drama. We are brought to a full realization of those surroundings because, in a series of scenes, each with their own intrinsic value as social comedy, or drama, we grow familiar with a number of households and their way of life, which is both individual and representative. There is, for instance, the financially precarious home life of the Tullivers themselves; Mr Tulliver speculative, perplexed and, compared with his wife, adventurous, and Mrs Tulliver, foolish and faithful, torn between loyalty to her own family and to the proud conventions of her Dodson upbringing. Then there are the prosperous middle-class homes of her sisters; Mrs Glegg's home at St Ogg's with its "front and back parlours so that she had two points of view from which she could observe the weakness of her fellow-beings, and reinforce her thankfulness for her own exceptional strength of mind," and the elegant home of Mrs Pullet with its "front door mats by no means intended to wipe shoes on: the very scraper had a deputy to do its dirty work"; and we are shown the well-conducted home life of Tom's ambitious clerical tutor, or, in contrast to all these, the home of Mr Tulliver's sister, Aunt Moss, who struggles to feed and clothe a large family on the proceeds of a farm starved of capital, since she had committed the indiscretion of marrying solely for love. All these aspects of life that the reader encounters as they impinge on Maggie's childhood, and that he relishes for their own vivid humour or pathos, convey the breadth of the world that surrounds an individual life and the narrowness of the space in which such a life can freely grow.

NOTE

2. Cross, vol. II, p. 262; from a letter to Blackwood replying to the criticism of Sir Edward Bulwer Lytton.

> —Joan Bennett, "Vision and Design." *Discussions of George Eliot*, ed. Richard Stang, (Boston: D.C. Heath and Company, 1960): 64–65.

SUZANNE GRAVER ON ELIOT'S VIEW OF TRAGEDY

[Suzanne Graver is John Hawley Roberts Professor of English at Williams College. She specializes in Victorian Literature and Women's Studies. She is the author of *George Eliot and Community: A Study in Social Theory and Fictional Form*, " ' Incarnate History': The Feminisms of Middlemarch," and "Writing in a 'Womanly' Way and the Double Vision of *Bleak House.*" Here she discusses Eliot's three major principles of tragedy and how they affect Maggie's moral evolution, illustrated by her relation to Stephen Guest.]

This conflict between "two irreconcilable requirements"—one of which speaks to "our individual needs," the other "to the dire necessities of our lot"—is for George Eliot quintessential to tragedy. She writes, "tragedy consists in the terrible difficulty," if not the impossibility, of creating "an adjustment ... between the individual and the general."[7] The former presupposes a telos focused on the individual; the latter, on society.

The shift in the portrait of Stephen from privileged gentleman to romantic lover enforces this view of tragedy. The more Stephen continues to be merely a coxcomb of good society, the less tenable the idea of a national life that is capable of sustaining a social telos. By minimizing Stephen's social status and emphasizing instead Maggie's inward struggle, George Eliot separates the outward social world from that which is inward or personal, allowing the claims of each to be presented as inviolate. This separation prepares, in turn, for the attempted resolution of the conflict between inward and outward at the close.

In addition to conflict and antithesis, George Eliot's view of tragedy includes two other major principles. One is that "a tragedy has not to expound why the individual must give way to the general; it has to show that it is compelled to give way; the tragedy consisting in the struggle involved, and often in the entirely calamitous issue in spite of a grand submission" (Cross, *George Eliot's Life* 3: 33). The end of the novel and a passage that appears only in the manuscript suggest, however, that while George Eliot thinks Maggie's story tragic, she also retreats from so calamitous a collision.[8] The excised passage, which originally appeared immediately after the first statement contrasting outward and inward, reads: "A girl ... may still hold forces within her as the living plant-seed does, which will make a way for themselves, often in a shattering, violent manner" (III, v, 208 [n. 7]). The action at the novel's end is "shattering," of course, but Maggie's response is not; no sooner does she know that the flood has come than she feels "a great calm" (VII, v, 451).

This sense of calm is the third aspect of George Eliot's definition of tragedy. Having spoken of how "the individual must give way to the general," she asks, "Now, what is the fact about our individual lots" in the face of "the commonest inherited misfortunes"? Her answer is:

> The utmost approach to well-being that can be made in such a case is through large resignation and acceptance of the inevitable, with as much effort to overcome any disadvantage as good sense will show to be attended with a likelihood of success. Any one may say, that is the dictate of mere rational reflection. But calm can, in hardly any human organism, be attained by rational reflection. Happily, we are not left to that. Love, pity, constituting sympathy, and generous joy with regard to the lot of our fellowmen comes in—has been growing since the beginning—enormously enhanced by wider vision of results, by all imagination actively interested in the lot of mankind generally; and these feelings become piety— *i.e.*, loving, willing submission and heroic Promethean effort

towards high possibilities, which may result from our individual life.

[Cross, *George Eliot's Life* 3: 33–34]

The turns and counterturns in this statement, particularly in the
light of the preceding comments about "irreparable collision"
and "calamitous issue," are dizzying and contradictory. The
irreconcilable antitheses George Eliot initially assigns to tragedy
are here replaced by a "calm" she associates with "love, pity," and
"sympathy ... with regard to the lot of our fellowmen."

George Eliot's desire to create this kind of affirmation at the
close of *The Mill on the Floss* bears directly on the change that
occurs in the depiction of Stephen. Whereas the forces that pull
Maggie to Stephen are presented as essentially inward, her
decision to leave him is presented as satisfying both her inward
needs and her sense of duty. Her decision reflects her love for
Tom, a family bond, and the love, pity, and sympathy she feels for
Lucy and Philip. This union of feelings corresponds to the
joining, in the passage above, of the "individual life" and the "lot
of our fellowmen." Thus it represents not the single telos that
defines her relation to Stephen but one that is double. Had
Stephen remained the representative of good society, the
indictment of the outward social world would have been so
severe as to have made impossible the novel's attempt to affirm a
social telos. Society comes off badly enough in the last book
because of the behavior of the "world's wife," but Maggie is
oblivious to this emblem in a way she could never be to Stephen.
Her acceptance of her duty to others depends in part on her
paying so little attention to what is said about her: again the
affirmation requires evasion.

Maggie's triumph over the world's wife by virtue of her moral
superiority participates in this pattern of evasion, for it requires
that Stephen continue to be portrayed in a good light. The
"heroism of renunciation," George Eliot points out elsewhere,
requires "that the thing we renounce is precious."[9] Accordingly,
to treat Stephen critically would be to devalue Maggie's
renunciation and her moral evolution. The more intense the
struggle within each becomes, the less can Stephen be depicted
as an "insolent coxcomb." He becomes ardent logician, instead,

opposing the love that is "natural" to "unnatural" social bonds. At the same time, as Maggie matures, love and social bonds become so intertwined within her as to make the one as natural as the other. In the end, it is Stephen's suffering and misery, in fact, that constitute the most "dire ... temptation to Maggie" (VII, v, 450). In her moral evolution there is "'an art which does mend nature'"—but not without injuring the art of the novel.

Most readers sense that Maggie's moral evolution is meant to represent that continuous adjustment of external to internal relations essential to social organicism.[10] Nonetheless, the process of adjustment in the closing chapters excludes a good part of what had earlier dissociated the outward from the inward in Maggie's life. In Books Four and Five, Maggie's turning to à Kempis clearly demonstrates that division. His "simple rule" requires the repudiation of earthly good; Maggie, however, initially adopts his rule because of the absence of earthly good from her life. Her longings for this good do not cease; thus, the solace she finds in à Kempis means at best a "negative peace," at worst, continued privation and starvation.[11] When à Kempis is reintroduced in Books Six and Seven, the critique of renunciation and the corresponding critique of society are absent. Renunciation, first presented as shutting out "'the avenues by which the life of your fellow-men might become known to you'" (V, iii, 286) is now identified with a "new force of unselfish human love" (VII, v, 449). If George Eliot is making a distinction between the "narrow valley of humiliation" of à Kempis's monastic rule and a Feuerbachian or Comtean commitment to sympathy with all that is human as opposed to divine, it is surely a distinction of which Maggie is unaware.

Some years before, in reviewing Mackay's *Progress of the Intellect*, George Eliot spoke of how "religion and philosophy" are "identical ... when root and branch exhibit the conditions of a healthy and vigorous life" (*Essays*, p. 31). The positive treatment of Maggie's final turning to à Kempis requires this kind of identification, but the repeated images of disease in the novel and the wish for death that accompanies Maggie's final prayer give the lie to "healthy and vigorous" growth. The mending of nature is forced, indeed, when the sense of duty that becomes second nature to Maggie compels a dying to self.

7. "Notes on *The Spanish Gypsy* and Tragedy in General," in Cross, *George Eliot's Life* 3: 30–35. See also "The Antigone and Its Moral," *Essays*, pp. 264–65.

8. *Letters* 3: 317; 374. See also 3: 269, where Lewes speaks of the "strain of poetry" that "relieve[s] the tragedy" at the close.

9. George Eliot is criticizing Geraldine Jewsbury for creating a character who renounced a man "'not worth the keeping'" (*Essays*, pp. 134–35). Stephen Guest, of course, has been criticized on similar grounds. The most famous attacks are by Leslie Stephen, who emphasizes the early portrait (*George Eliot*, pp. 100–104), and by Leavis, who argues that Stephen is not worthy of Maggie's "spiritual and idealistic nature" though neither character nor author realize it (*Great Tradition*, pp. 43–46).

10. See chapter 4 above, pp. 152–53.

11. *MF*, V, iii, 284–88; VI, iii, 336.

<blockquote>—Suzanne Graver, George Eliot and Community: A Study in Social Theory and Fictional Form, (Berkeley: University of California Press, 1984): 194–197.</blockquote>

U.C. Knoepflmacher on the Clash of Present and Future

[U.C. Knoepflmacher is Professor of English at Princeton University. He is the author of *Ventures into Childland* and the editor of *Forbidden Journeys* and *Endurance of Frankenstein*.]

Mr. Tulliver's story introduces all the basic collisions of the novel: the antithesis between the worlds of the Mill by the Ripple and of St. Ogg's-on-the-Floss, the contrast between Dodsons and Tullivers, the resulting oppositions between parents and children, brother and sister, and Maggie's consequent self-division. Yet the unit which ends with the miller's deathbed recognition that the "world's been too many" for him, possesses the tragic requisites which the remainder of the novel lacks. Like Oedipus, to whom he is compared by the narrator, Mr. Tulliver has become entangled in "the skein of life" through his own blind pride. Unlike the symbolic flood which executes Tom and

Maggie, the catastrophe which marks his downfall is the direct result of the interaction of character and destiny, will and fate. Mr. Tulliver falls victim to his own faulty choices. He first selects a spouse for her presumed submissiveness and stupidity; then, betrayed by the unexpected biological "crossing o' breeds," he prefers his Tulliver daughter over his Dodson son. To prepare for Tom's future, he chooses a "gentleman's" education which is as unprofitable as that of Amos Barton or Dickens' Pip; he adopts the advice of Mr. Riley instead of enlisting the better judgment of Mr. Deane, his brother-in-law, whom he regards as "the 'knowingest' man of his acquaintance," but whom he does not consult on family matters because of vanity and pride. Able to avoid a costly litigation, the imprudent miller opts a lawsuit instead and thus finally places himself in the power of Chancery, that Victorian embodiment of ancient "Fortuna." Incapable of adapting to the changes taking place around him, he escapes, as Maggie will, into rebellion, fantasy, and, eventually, death. Unlike his daughter, however, he is far more the victim of his own hubris than of capricious chance.

Mr. Deane is the miller's exact counterpart. A self-made city man, he knows the ways of the world. The foolish Mr. Tulliver congratulates himself for having chosen a classicist as Tom's teacher. Always impulsive, he soon convinces himself that the boy's tutor is a "clergyman whose knowledge was so applicable to the everyday affairs of this life. Except Counsellor Wylde, whom he had heard at the last session, Mr. Tulliver thought the Rev. Mr. Stelling was the shrewdest fellow he had ever met with—not unlike Wylde, in fact: he had the same way of sticking his thumbs in the armholes of his waistcoat" (Bk. II, chap. 1, p. 211). The utilitarian Mr. Deane, on the other hand, soon brands Tom's education as utterly useless. Even after the youth pathetically promises to unlearn his Latin and ancient history, Mr. Deane presses on contemptuously: "Your Latin and rigmarole may soon dry off you, but you'll be but a bare stick after that. Besides, it's whitened your hands and taken the rough work out of you. And what do you know? Why, you know nothing about book-keeping, to begin with, and not so much of reckoning as a common shopman. You'll have to begin at the low round of the ladder, let me tell you, if you mean to get on in life. It's no use forgetting the education your father's been paying for, if you don't give yourself a new un." (Bk. III, chap. 5, pp. 361–362.) Ironically, the very man whose advice Mr. Tulliver shunned, now teaches his Dodson son how to repair the father's mistakes.

Mr. Deane typifies the new ways of St. Ogg's. Like Lawyer Wakem, he plays Octavius to Mr. Tulliver's Antony. The miller who gallops incessantly around his threatened land is impulsive and sentimental; his unlanded brother-in-law exerts himself only by "taking snuff vigorously, as he always did when wishing to maintain a neutral position" (Bk. I, chap. 7, p. 105). Like Wakem, Mr. Deane remains evasive and noncommittal. Whereas Mr. Tulliver identifies his archenemy with "old Harry" himself, Mr. Deane cautiously respects Lawyer Wakem as a powerful business rival. Mr. Tulliver vows that he will not allow "anybody get hold of his whip-hand" (Bk. I, chap. 5, p. 53), but when he loses control of his lands, it is his brother-in-law who asks the stricken miller to accept Wakem's demeaning offer to let him manage the property he formerly owned. Mr. Deane could easily have outbid the lawyer in order to salvage Mr. Tulliver's pride, but he does not "carry on business on sentimental grounds" (Bk. III, chap. 7, p. 383). In his unromantic world a man can succeed only by waiting patiently, as he has done, "before he got the whip in his hand" (Bk. VI, chap. 5, p. 200). If the descendant of the fiery Ralph Tulliver rides against the times, his prudent counterpart moves with the tide. Once regarded as the worst match made by the Dodson sisters, Mr. Deane has gradually risen to eminence in the Guests' "great mill-owning, ship-owning business." Progress is his motto as much as it is that of Dickens' Podsnap or Gradgrind: "I don't find fault with the change, as some people do. Trade, sir, opens a man's eyes; and if population is to get thicker upon the ground, as it's doing, the world must use its wits at inventions of some sort or other." (Bk. VI, chap. 5, p. 201.)

While Mr. Tulliver loses control of his mill wheel by entering useless litigations over his decreasing "water-power," the self-controlled Mr. Deane steadily gains in influence by harnessing new sources of power: "It's this steam, you see, that has made the difference: it drives on every wheel double pace, and the wheel of fortune along with 'em, as our Mr. Stephen Guest said." (Bk. VI, chap. 5, p. 201). If Mr. Tulliver is the enfeebled survivor of

Carlyle's "Heroical Age," Mr. Deane belongs to the new mechanical era "which, with its whole undivided might, forwards, teaches, and practices the great art of adapting means to ends."[34] Deane's sphere of action seems every bit as removed from Dorlcote Mill as Caesar's Rome is from Cleopatra's Egypt. At the mill, the relation between Luke and his master still resembles that of a vassal and his feudal lord; Luke's loyalty is not unlike the devotion of a Kent or Enobarbus. For the world soon to be lost by the miller is archaic enough to harbor what Hegel had called "romantic fidelity."[35] In it the ideal of service remains as untouched as the urge for revenge which dominates the "pagan" Mr. Tulliver and his son. Like old Adam in *As You Like It*, Luke wants to give his earnings to his master, for he feels, "after the manner of contented hard-working men whose lives have been spent in servitude, that sense of natural fitness in rank which made his master's downfall a tragedy to him" (Bk. III, chap. 8, p. 405).

NOTES

34. "Signs of the Times," *Critical and Miscellaneous Essays*, I, *The Complete Works of Thomas Carlyle* (New York, 1901), p. 465.

35. Cf. Hegel's discussion of dramatic motivation in *Aesthetik*. Citing the swineherd's loyalty to Ulysses and Kent's loyalty to Lear, he comments: "This borders as close as possible on that which we would make clear as romantic fidelity. Fidelity at this stage is not the loyalty of slaves and churls ... [but] the liege-service of chivalry, in which each vassal preserves his own free self-dependence as an essential element in the attitude of subordination to one of higher rank, whether lord, king, or emperor. This type of fidelity ... forms the fundamental bond of union in a common [i.e., communal] society" (*Hegel on Tragedy*, ed. Anne and Henry Paolucci [New York, 1962], p. 204).

—U.C. Knoepflmacher, *George Eliot's Early Novels: The Limits of Realism*, (Berkeley: University of California Press, 1968): 194–198.

Silas Marner

With *Silas Marner*, Eliot turned her attention away from her own childhood memories toward a more allegorical story of an outsider whose lost faith, nursed by his love of material wealth, eventually is restored by love and the milk of human kindness. Throughout the narrative run themes of blackmail and deceit, fatherhood and redemption.

For fifteen years, the misanthropic weaver Silas Marner has lived in Raveloe, a provincial Midland village whose people are prone to superstition and unaccepting of newcomers. Before Silas arrived, he lived an artisan's life in the narrowly religious Lantern Yard, where he was engaged to a young servant woman and thought he had a loyal confidant in friend William Dane. But Silas' inexplicable cataleptic fits aroused suspicion, especially in Dane, who framed Silas for stealing church money and later stole his fiancée, forcing Silas to flee to Raveloe in pain and disbelief. In the following years, until the opening of the narrative, Silas concentrated only on weaving sixteen hours a day and hoarding his gold. His knowledge of herbal remedies, displayed once when he relieved the cobbler's wife with foxglove, aroused further suspicion from the citizens of Raveloe.

Godfrey Cass, the good-natured eldest son of Squire Cass, the richest man in Raveloe, was given rent money for his father; against his better judgment, he lent it to his gambling-prone younger brother, Dunstan. Now that rent has come due, Godfrey pleads Dunstan to recover the money. Dunstan, sneering, threatens to expose Godfrey's secret marriage to the opium-addicted Molly Farren, the revelation of which would both alienate the Squire and Godfrey's love interest, Nancy Lammeter. Finally, Dunstan agrees to sell Godfrey's horse, Wildfire, at a fair. On his way, he manages to sell the horse, but then stakes and accidentally kills it. Distraught and drunk, Dunstan wanders into Silas's cottage and, remembering the weaver has a hoard, finds the gold and disappears.

Silas returns and finds his hoard missing. Aghast, he notifies the Raveloe citizens at the Rainbow pub. The weaver is so upset that the townsfolk believe his story; they suggest a suspicious-looking peddler may be the culprit, using a tinderbox found outside Silas's cottage as further evidence. Members of the community, especially Dolly Winthrop, the wheelwright's wife, take pity on Silas, but he can neither be comforted nor coaxed back into society.

When time passes without the return of Dunstan, Godfrey confesses his misdeeds to his disapproving father and tells him of his love for Nancy Lammeter. At their New Year's Party on his father's estate, the Red House, Godfrey speaks to Nancy, who seems cold and chagrined. Molly Farren, wishing for recognition and revenge, journeys through the falling snow to appear at the party. On the way, she falls into the snow and dies in front of Silas's house, while the weaver is caught in a fit of unconsciousness. Her child sees the bright light in Silas's cottage, wanders in, and falls asleep before his hearth. When he awakens, he sees the child's golden hair on the floor and thinks his gold has returned to him; coming to his senses, he ventures to the Squire's house with the news, cradling Godfrey's own child in his arms. Godfrey accompanies the group back to Silas' cottage, and seeing Molly, he is relieved that he can now marry Nancy and resolved to keep his past a secret. But guilt prompts Godfrey to provide money to clothe the child. Silas names the child Hephzibah, or Eppie, after his mother and younger sister, and resolves to keep her.

Sixteen years later, Eppie has flourished under Silas' thoughtful care and the friendship of Dolly Winthrop and her son, Aaron. Silas, in turn, has found meaning in life through Eppie. Godfrey has continued to support Eppie and has married Nancy, who is unable to bear children; Dustan has not returned. Eppie reveals that Aaron Winthrop has proposed to her and that the new couple plans to live with Silas. Mentioning the successful example of Eppie's adoption, Godfrey suggests to Nancy that they might adopt a child, but Nancy refuses, saying doing so would be to meddle with the wishes of Providence. Dunstan's skeleton, along with Marner's gold, is found in the stone-pits next to Silas's cottage. Realizing that all comes to light eventually, Godfrey confesses his previous marriage and fatherhood to

Nancy. Nancy's only regret is that they haven't adopted Eppie sooner; the couple visits the cottage that evening and suggests Eppie comes to live with them. She refuses, stating her allegiance to the weaver. When Godfrey admits that he is Eppie's natural father, and that he has repented, Eppie still insists upon staying. Five days later, Eppie and Silas make a visit to Lantern Yard and find it utterly transformed. Silas realizes that his only home is Raveloe. The story concludes with the wedding of Eppie and Aaron, with a dress provided by Nancy and a procession past the Red House.

Silas Marner

Silas Marner is a weaver who, falsely accused of committing a crime, was forced to leave his home in Lantern Yard for the village of Raveloe. Frustrated with religion and humanity, his only solace is the accumulation of wealth through work, until the appearance of a wayward child on his hearth gives his life new meaning.

The adopted daughter of Silas Marner, **Eppie** is actually the biological child of Godfrey Cass and Molly Farren, his estranged wife. She grows up under the doting eye of Silas, and even when her biological father and his new wife offer to give her a more comfortable life, she elects to stay with the weaver.

The eldest son of the wealthy Squire Cass, **Godfrey Cass** is well-meaning despite his occasionally questionable morals. He is in love with Nancy Lammeter, but because his estranged wife, Molly, is still living, he can't marry her.

Dunstan Cass is Godfrey's younger brother. Prone to stealing, drinking, and gambling, he accidentally kills Godfrey's horse, which he is on his way to sell; after stealing money from Silas' cottage, he is never heard from again.

Molly Farren is Godfrey Cass's wife and the mother of his child. In a fit of vengeance over the fact that Godfrey said he'd rather die than acknowledge her, she journeys to his father's New Year's Eve party in the snow, but dies on the way.

The object of Godfrey's affections and his eventual wife, **Nancy Lammeter**, the daughter of a good, country family, is beautiful and fastidious, though somewhat uneducated.

The wheelwright's wife who helps Silas, **Dolly Winthrop** later becomes Eppie's mother-in-law.

Aaron Winthrop is Dolly's son and Eppie's eventual husband.

Silas Marner

JEROME THALE ON THE PARALLEL STORIES OF GODFREY AND SILAS

[Jerome Thale is the author of "The Paradox of Individualism: Middlemarch." Here, he argues that the story of Godfrey Cass is simply the story of Silas Marner, set in a minor key.]

The Silas story, taken by itself, offers us immensely more hope and reassurance than any other of her novels, but it does so less convincingly. The belief in goodness of heart, the belief that nature never did betray, are totally unexamined. It is true that there is some equity in that Silas's suffering is compensated for by his happiness with Eppie. But this happiness comes about only as the result of a chance, or as Silas sees it, a miracle. In an extra-natural account of reality it is possible to accept chance as a symbol, expressive of providence or of beneficent order in the universe. For we allow faith to supplement and sometimes supersede an experiential account of the world. It is of course just this that Silas does. He comes to accept a reassuring view of life, embodied for him in the Church of England; and in this scheme Eppie's coming is not a miracle as he first thought but part of the working of Providence (the miracle is its own evidence for its miraculousness). But the naturalistic presuppositions of the novel, the reduction of everything to the facts of experience, rule out any such providential view of human affairs. Silas is restored and believes, but can those who do not have Silas's good luck see the universe as harmonious and beneficent, see good as conquering evil and dullness? What happens to the simple-minded Silas gives him grounds for trusting, but it seems to offer a critical mind no particular grounds for trusting, believing, or loving.

This may seem to be taking unfair advantage of the novel by applying realistic criteria to an incident which is part of a fairy tale. Certainly the coincidence and the happy ending do not bother us; they are familiar enough in literature. What does bother us is that the coincidence must stand as some sort of proof or justification for Silas's view of a providential and harmonious working of the universe at the same time that the novel works in a realistic framework of strict probability in which coincidence is forbidden as a distortion of reality. Should we say, then, that the use of coincidence is an artistic defect stemming from the expression of a vain hope?

One does not like to suppose that George Eliot meant to give us a fairy tale as a serious reflection of life. We can hardly think that like Mrs. Browning or Charlotte M. Yonge she could deliberately confound or could not distinguish between wishes and the facts of experience.

The rest of George Eliot's work, with its disenchantment, is a relevant argument here. It also is evidence for the seriousness of her concern with the problem of what kind of sense of the world our experience justifies. To resolve the antinomy at which we have arrived and see in what way we must take the Silas story, we must think of it as only one half of a novel, the other half of which is the Godfrey story.

The stories are related in a parallel and complementary way. The fortunes of the two men alternate, and there is a series of pairings in character and situation. Godfrey refuses a blessing and is unhappy. Silas accepts it and is made happy. Just as Godfrey has two wives, so Silas has two treasures, and each of the two men is a father to Eppie. Godfrey is betrayed by his brother Dunstan, Silas by his friend William Dane. Godfrey is secretly guilty, Silas secretly innocent. Dunstan and the gold are buried together, for the gold is Silas's undoing and the blackmailing brother is Godfrey's. When the gold and Dunstan's body are brought to light it is for Silas's joy and Godfrey's shame. Gold passes from Silas to the Casses, Eppie from the Casses to Silas.

All these parallels and contrasts indicate the care with which the novel as a whole is worked out; more significantly, they point to the fact that the two stories involve the same theme, that Godfrey's story is Silas's transposed into a minor key. Godfrey like Silas is alienated from himself and from society. He endures a period of desolation almost as long as Silas's—fifteen years— not warped and isolated as Silas is, but incapable of happiness, uneasy over his deceit and his failure to acknowledge his daughter. Silas's exile ends when Godfrey's begins, and the transfer of the golden-haired child is symbolic. The general pattern of the two stories is identical, but for Godfrey there is no happy ending.

The point of the thematic parallelism becomes clear when we think of the contrast in tonality between the two stories. Remembering the Silas story we think of the fire on the hearth, the golden-haired girl, the sunny days, the garden, the bashful suitor. Even in his desolation Silas is seen against a pastoral landscape. Compare the introduction of Godfrey:

> It was the once hopeful Godfrey who was standing, with his hands in his side-pockets and his back to the fire, in the dark wainscoted parlour, one late November afternoon.... The fading grey light fell dimly on the walls decorated with guns, whips, and foxes' brushes, on coats and hats flung on the chairs, on tankards sending forth a scent of flat ale, and on a half-choked fire, with pipes propped up in the chimney-corners: signs of a domestic life destitute of any hallowing charm, with which the look of gloomy vexation on Godfrey's blond face was in sad accordance.

All through the Godfrey story the atmosphere is dull and oppressive. The story opens with Godfrey deprived of any prospect of happiness by his marriage to a dissipated barmaid, caught unable to replace his father's money which he has given to Dunstan, and threatened with exposure by both his brother and his wife. The story ends with Godfrey absenting himself from Raveloe on the wedding day of the daughter who has rejected him. In the years between there is the guilt and self-reproach over abandoning Eppie and deceiving his wife, there is Nancy and Godfrey's childlessness, and Nancy herself, narrow, barren, just dissatisfied. Even the minor figures in Godfrey's story are unhappy: the old squire is vaguely discontented, indulgent and resentful, a figure of quiet misery. It is a world greyed throughout, given up to "the vague dulness of the grey hours." No one is acutely unhappy as Silas is, but they are people who seem to sense that they are never to have much joy, that their usual happiness is the absence of pain.

Of course, the difference between the two stories is proper enough since one is a fairy tale and the other a piece done in George Eliot's usual disenchanted realism. But this only describes the difference and does not account for it, does not tell us why the two stories are brought together, what the juxtaposition of two such different views of life means.

> —Jerome Thale, "George Eliot's Fable for Her Times: *Silas Marner*," *Discussions of George Eliot*, ed. Richard Stang, (Boston: D.C. Heath and Company, 1960): 97–99.

SANDRA M. GILBERT ON THE SIGNIFICANCE OF DAUGHTERHOOD

[Sandra M. Gilbert is Professor of English at the University of California, Davis. With Susan Gubar she co-wrote *The Madwoman in the Attic: The Woman Writer and the Nineteenth-Century Literary Imagination* and the *Norton Anthology of Literature by Women*. She's also published more than forty poems and essays. Here, she discusses how Eppie is affected by having such an effect on Silas.]

What does it mean to Eppie to mean all this for Silas? Certainly Eliot had long been concerned with the social significance and cultural possibilities of daughterhood. Both *The Mill on the Floss*—the novel that precedes *Silas Marner*—and *Romola*—the one that follows it—are elaborate examinations of the structural inadequacies of a daughter's estate. As for Marian Evans, moreover, her real life had persistently confronted her with the problematic nature of daughterhood and its corollary condition, sisterhood. As biographers have shown, her feelings for her own father were ambivalent not only during his lifetime but throughout hers; yet his superegoistic legacy pervaded other relationships she formed. When she was in her early twenties, for instance, she became a dutiful disciple to the Casaubon-like Dr Brabant, who 'punningly baptized her *Deutera* because she was to be a second daughter to him'.[24] And even when she was a middle-aged woman, she remembered her older brother Isaac as a kind of miniature father, 'a Like unlike, a Self that self restrains', observing wistfully that 'were another childhood-world my share, / I would be born a little sister there'.[25] Since 'Eppie' was the name of Silas' little sister, it seems likely that, in being 'born' again to the mild weaver, Marian Evans did in fiction if not in fact re-create herself as both daughter and little sister.

Certainly Eppie's protestations of daughterly devotion suggest that she is in some sense a born-again daughter. 'I should have no delight i' life any more if I was forced to go away from my father,' she tells Nancy and Godfrey Cass (*SM*, 2. 19). Like the Marian Evans who became 'Deutera', Eppie is not so much a second daughter as twice a daughter—a doubly daughterly daughter. As such a 'Deutera', she is the golden girl whose being reiterates those cultural commandments Moses set forth for the second time in Deuteronomy. Thus, although scrupulous Nancy Lammeter Cass has often been seen as articulating Eliot's moral position on the key events of this novel, it is really the more impulsive Eppie who is the conscience of the book.

This becomes clearest when Nancy argues that 'there's a duty you owe to your lawful father'. Eppie's instant reply, with its counterclaim that 'I can't feel as I've got any father but one', expresses a more accurate understanding of the idea of fatherhood (*SM*, 2. 19). For in repudiating *God-free* Cass, who is only by chance (*casus*) her natural father, and affirming Silas Marner, who is by choice her cultural father, Eppie rejects the lawless father in favor of the lawful one, indicating her clear awareness that fatherhood itself is both *a* social construct (or, in Stephen Dedalus' words, 'a legal fiction') and *the* social construct that constructs society.[26] Having achieved and acted on this analysis, she is rewarded with a domestic happiness which seems to prove Dickinson's contention that it is 'vain to punish Honey, / It only sweeter grows'. At the same time, in speaking such a law, this creature of milk and honey initiates the re-education and redemption of Godfrey Cass: the cultural code of Deuteronomy speaks through her, suggesting that, even if she is a Christmas child, she is as much a daughter of the Old Testament as of the New, of the first telling of the law as of its second telling.[27]

Happy and dutiful as she is, however, Eppie is not perfectly contented, for she has a small fund of anxiety that is pledged to her other parent—her lost mother. This intermittent sadness, which manifests itself as a preoccupation with her mother's wedding ring, directs our attention to a strange disruption at the center of *Silas Marner*: the history of Eppie's dead mother. On the surface, of course, the ring that Silas has saved for his adopted daughter is an aptly ironic symbol of that repressed plot, since there never was any bond beyond an artificial one between Molly Farren and Godfrey Cass, the lawless father 'of whom [the ring] was the symbol'. But Eppie's frequent ruminations on the questions of 'how her mother looked, whom she was like, and how [Silas] had found her against the furze bush' suggest that there is something more problematic than a traditional bad marriage at issue here (*SM*, 2. 16). As so often in this 'legendary tale', what seems like a moral point also offers an eerily accurate account of what Freud sees as the inexorable psychosexual growth and entry of the daughter into a culture shaped by the codes of the father. 'Our insight into [the pre-Oedipus] phase in the little girl's development comes to us as a surprise, comparable ... with ... the discovery of the Minoan–Mycenaean civilization behind that of Greece', remarks Freud, explaining that 'everything connected with this first mother-attachment has ... seemed to me ... lost in a past so dim and shadowy ... that it seemed as if it had undergone some specially inexorable repression'.[28]

Indeed, Molly Farren *has* undergone a 'specially inexorable repression' in this novel. Three or four pages of a single chapter are devoted to her, though her damned and doomed wanderings in the snow strikingly recapitulate the lengthier wanderings of fallen women like Hetty Sorrel and Maggie Tulliver. I suggest that Eliot attempts this drastic condensation precisely because *Silas Marner*, in allowing her to speak symbolically about the meaning of daughterhood, also allowed her to speak in even more resonant symbols about the significance of motherhood. What she said was what she saw: that it is better to be a daughter than a mother and better still to be a father than a daughter. For when the Deuteronomy of culture formulates the incest laws that lie at the center of human society, that severe code tells the son: 'You may not have your mother; you may not kill your father.' But when it is translated into a 'Daughteronomy' preached for the growing girl, it says: 'You must bury your mother; you must give yourself to your father.'[29] Since the daughter has inherited an empty pack and cannot *be* a father, she has no choice but to be *for* the father—to be his treasure, his land, his voice.

Yet, as Eliot shows, the growing girl is haunted by her own difficult passage from mother to father, haunted by the primal scene in the snow when she was forced to turn away from the body of the mother, the emblem of nature which can give only so much and no more, and seek the hearth of the father, the emblem of culture that must compensate for nature's inadequacies.[30] This moment is frozen into the center of *Silas Marner* like the dead figure of Molly Farren Cass, whose final posture of self-abandonment brings about Eppie's 'effort to regain the pillowing arm and bosom; but mammy's ear was deaf, and the pillow seemed to be slipping away backward' (*SM*, 1. 12). Indeed, for women the myth that governs personality may be based on such a moment, a confrontation of the dead mother that is as enduring and horrifying to daughters as Freud (in *Totem and Taboo*) claimed the nightmare of the dead father was to sons. Finally, the garden that Eppie and Silas plant at the end of the novel memorializes this moment. '"Father",' says the girl 'in a tone of gentle gravity ..., "we shall take the furze bush into the garden"'—for it was against the bush that Molly died (*SM*, 2. 16). Now, fenced in by the garden of the law, the once 'straggling' bush will become a symbol of nature made meaningful, controlled and confined by culture (*SM*, 1. 12).

NOTES

24. HAIGHT, *George Eliot*, p. 49.

25. ELIOT, 'Brother and Sister', *The Poems of George Eliot* (New York, n.d.), pp. 356, 357.

26. JAMES JOYCE, *Ulysses* (New York, 1934), p. 205; on the significance of the name 'Cass', see Knoepflmacher, *George Eliot's Early Novels*, p. 239.

27. Because of her metonymic as well as coincidental connection with the gold stolen by Godfrey Cass' brother Dunstan, Eppie represents the law in yet another way, reinforcing our sense that its curses as well as its blessings cannot be averted. The place in society that Silas' false brother, William *Dane*, stole from him is ironically restored

to him through an act of theft perpetrated by Godfrey's false brother, *Dunstan* Cass. Though he has tried to flee culture on the horse Wildfire, moreover, Dunstan falls inexorably into the Stone-pits of damnation— the abyss the law has prepared for him. Similarly, his God-free brother, who tries to flee his cultural responsibility as father, loses not one but all children and inherits an empty house, a mere shell or box (a 'case', so to speak) devoid of meaning because devoid both of sons who can carry on its name and daughters who can link it into society. Even his refusal to be his prodigal brother's keeper eventually brings about Godfrey's nemesis, for it is the discovery of Dunstan's skeleton in the Stone-pits that causes this rejecting father to make his rejected proposal to Eppie. In all these cases, essentially, the machinations of murderous brothers dramatize failures of just those Mosaic Laws of the Father which should make transactions between man and man both orderly and faithful.

28. FREUD, 'Female Sexuality' (1931), trans. Joan Riviere, *Sexuality and the Psychology of Love*, p. 195; all further references to this work, abbreviated 'FS', will be included in the text.

29. According to Freud, the Oedipus complex means for the girl an attachment to the father which parallels the boy's attachment to his mother; but for the girl, her attachment to the father is a 'positive' phenomenon that succeeds an earlier 'negative' phase in which she experiences the same 'first mother-attachment' that the boy feels. When the girl learns that her mother has not 'given' her a penis, however— i.e., in Lacan's sense, that the mother has not given her the power represented by the 'Phallus'—she turns in disgust and despair to the father, the one who has the phallus and may therefore be able to give her some of its power (see Freud, 'FS', pp. 195, 199, and passim, and 'Some Psychological Consequences of the Anatomical Distinction between the Sexes'). Interestingly in this regard, Sadoff observes that a 'pattern of the displaced mother occurs throughout Eliot's novels and serves the story of father–daughter seduction' (*Monsters of Affection*, p. 69).

30. Observing that 'a boy's repression of his Oedipal maternal attachment (and his pre-oedipal dependence) seems to be *more* complete than a girl's'—in part, no doubt, because the boy can look forward to a future in which he will 'have' at least a figure of the mother, Chodorow quotes Alice Balint's assertion that 'the amicable loosening of the bond between daughter and mother is one of the most difficult tasks of education' (*The Reproduction of Mothering*, p. 130).

—Sandra M. Gilbert, "Life's Empty Pack: Notes Toward a Literary Daughteronomy." *George Eliot*, ed. K.M. Newton, (New York: Longman Group, 1991): 106–109.

[Meri-Jane Rochelson is Associate Professor of English
at Florida International University. She is the editor of
Children of the Ghetto and the co-editor of *Transforming
Genres: New Approaches to British Fiction of the 1890s.* Here
she explores how Eliot's use of metaphor and variation of
narrative perspective informs the reader of *Silas Marner.*]

Many critics have commented on the way Eliot frequently shifts
the perspective of her narrative, like the changing or refocusing
of a lens,[6] and she does so in the following passage early in *Silas
Marner.* The narrator begins at a medium distance: "And what
could be more unlike that Lantern Yard world than the world of
Raveloe?—orchards looking lazy with neglected plenty; the large
church in the wide churchyard, which men gazed at lounging at
their own doors in service-time; the purple-faced farmers
jogging along the lanes or turning in at the Rainbow;
homesteads, where men supped heavily and slept in the light of
the evening hearth, and where women seemed to be laying up a
stock of linen for the life to come."[7] The narrator describes
Raveloe as an objective traveler might, surveying its landscape
and inhabitants from sufficiently near to infer its complacent
abundance, but at a distance that still prevents intimate
acquaintance. The picture is in many ways inviting, but the
remote perspective suggests a coolness or aloofness which is, in
fact, confirmed in the second sentence: "there were no lips in
Raveloe from which a word could fall that would stir Silas
Marner's benumbed faith to a sense of pain." The narrator's view
moves closer in, to Silas, and we see that his soul remains
untouched by the bounty and activity around him.

There has not been much metaphor in this section so far, so
that when it does appear—in the reference to a word that might
"Stir ... benumbed faith"—its effect is the more dramatic.
Analogies have appeared in the paragraph to this point: the
orchards "look" lazy, and the women only "seem to be" storing
linen for the afterlife. These comparisons help assure the reader

of the narrator's perceptive eye, and the content of the second is appropriate to the discussion of faith and varieties of belief that make up the subject of the passage. But that they are straightforward analogies, drawing attention through their form to the fact that the narrator is creating them and that the reality they illuminate is quite ordinary reality, makes one feel, too, how strongly the narrator is in control. This feeling that one is being led along by a calm, perceptive, controlled narrator contributes as much to one's sense of the comfort of Raveloe as the actual images themselves. It is thus not only the shift in perspective but also the shift to metaphor, that accounts for the discomfort produced by the sentence about Silas. His faith does not "seem" numb; it *is* numb, and it must be awakened to pain when it begins to feel. (...)

The movement from one means of explanation to another conveys the earnestness of the narrator's desire to explain, and at the same time suggests that nothing can be explained through only a simple presentation of the data. The narrator then makes clear that the shift in perspective (from Raveloe to Silas, from survey to community to analysis of character) and the shift in rhetoric (from literal speech, to analogy, to metaphor) are still not enough to make the reader understand just what Silas Marner is experiencing. The sentence about Silas's benumbed faith is therefore followed by another shift in perspective: "In the early ages of the world, we know, it was believed that each territory was inhabited and ruled by its own divinities, so that a man could cross the bordering heights and be out of reach of his native gods, whose presence was confined to the streams and the groves and the hills among which he had lived from his birth. And poor Silas was vaguely conscious of something not unlike the feeling of primitive men, when they fled thus, in fear or in sulleness, from the face of an unpropitious deity."

The wider view provides a comparison between Silas's plight and the lives of "primitive men," and results from the same philosophical impulse as the employment of analogy and metaphor. What the narrator suggests is that fullness of understanding can only be approached if one compares the situation at hand to other situations like it. At base is the idea that all things can be related; as readers, we feel the narrator to be someone who sees in the world a unity between the petty details of life and the cosmic beliefs of ancient men, who cannot tell the story of one weaver without joining it to the lives of all people in all time.[10] We also sense the narrator's erudition in the fact that she knows about primitive men and their gods; our faith in her reliability as guide and interpreter increases as we appreciate her wisdom. We are impressed by her compassion in going to such lengths to make sure we understand what she is saying, and we are flattered that this wise, all-seeing narrator assumes "we know," as she does, all about ancient religion.

The brief explanation of local deities is presented as a simple, literal, matter of fact. Having already established her own reliability, the narrator thus places the reader in an attitude of respect toward something he might otherwise have treated with some scorn. He is then prepared to sympathize with Silas in his loss of faith. But in a subtle way this particular analogy also prepares the reader to reject, along with the primitive superstitions, certain forms of Christian belief which Eliot is to supplant in the novel with a religion of human compassion. The images of primitive gods take their place beside the lots-drawing of Lantern Yard in a system of references throughout the novel to superstitious faiths whose foundations may be false but whose believers are sincere.

The comparison between Silas and the early believers is stated explicitly, and as the paragraph ends the narrator reminds us of the more immediate comparison with which it began, the contrast between Raveloe and Lantern Yard: "It seemed to him that the Power he had vainly trusted in among the streets and at the prayer-meetings, was very far away from this land in which he had taken refuge, where men lived in careless abundance, knowing and needing nothing of that trust, which, for him, had been turned to bitterness." All the strands of explanation gradually come together here, in a powerful, simple metaphor. The sense of the whole paragraph is finally epitomized in the last sentence of the passage, an example of the "summary metaphor" that characterizes Eliot's narrator's rhetoric. By its very existence as metaphor, this statement adds something to the narration that could not have been rendered exactly any other way: "The little light he possessed spread its beams so narrowly, that frustrated belief was a curtain broad enough to create for him the blackness of night."

This sentence moves from light to darkness as the chapter so far has moved from the spiritual brightness of Silas's early life to the blankness of his later existence. In the "blackness of night" we have the clearest presentation yet of just how desolate his spiritual state is. With the metaphor, a "curtain" comes down on the bright and active scene of Raveloe life; it is blotted out for the reader just as, for Silas, the benevolent possibilities of that life are made invisible by his disillusionment. It is as if the narrator knows the reader cannot truly understand Silas's plight unless he has all the facts, and through every possible means. If we understand the narrowness of his "light," we will not be too impatient with Silas when frustration removes it completely. And in taking such a well-worn metaphor as the "light of faith" and transforming it into a physical light one may possess—a feeble, useless light, at that—the narrator reveals the pathos of Silas Marner's situation while at the same time suggesting the homely, personal quality of faith. We are led to speculate as to the solace a faith might provide, were its light only wide enough.

NOTES

6. An especially perceptive analysis of the technique may be found in Elizabeth Ermarth's essay "Method and Moral in George Eliot's Narrative," *Victorian Newsletter*, No. 47 (Spring 1975), 4–7.

7. George Eliot, *Silas Marner: The Weaver of Raveloe*, ed. Q. D. Leavis (Harmondsworth: Penguin, 1967), Chapter II, pp. 63–64. All subsequent references in text are to this edition.

10. This belief in analogy as the basis for understanding finds support in George Eliot's essays as well as in her novels. In "The Future of German Philosophy," a review of Otto Friedrich Gruppe's *Gegenwart und Zukunft der Philosophie in Deutschland*, Eliot affirmed her agreement with Gruppe that abstract ideas must be attained "by an ascent from positive particulars." Abstractions arise from perceptions or judgments, she writes, and "every judgment exhibits itself as a comparison, or perception of likeness in the midst of difference: the metaphor is no mere ornament of speech, but belongs to its essence" (*Leader*, 6 [1855], 723–24; rpt. in *Essays of George Eliot*, ed. Thomas Pinney [New York: Columbia University Press, 1963], pp. 152, 151).

—Meri-Jane Rochelson, "The Weaver of Raveloe: Metaphor as Narrative Persuasion in *Silas Marner.*" *The Critical Response to George Eliot*, ed. Karen L. Pangallo, (Westport, Connecticut: Greenwood Press, 1994): 100–103

ALEXANDER WELSH ON THE CASS BROTHERS AND BLACKMAIL

[Alexander Welsh is Emily Sanford Professor of English at Yale University. From 1975 to 1981 he edited *Nineteenth-Century Fiction*, the journal devoted to British and American fiction. He is the author of *From Copyright to Copperfield, Dickens Redressed: The Art of "Bleak House" and "Hard Times," Reflections on the Hero as Quixote, and Strong Representations: Narrative and Circumstantial Evidence in England.* Here he explores how blackmail figures into the relationship between Godfrey and Dunstan Cass.]

Though *Silas Marner* is a much more serious work than "Brother Jacob," the story of Godfrey Cass and his brother Dunstan is less serious at first than that of Marner. The narrator scorns the divided life of Godfrey, with his secret marriage that has taken place before the present action of the novel, as "an ugly story of low passion, delusion, and waking from delusion" and characterizes it as "vicious folly." She also refers to "a movement of compunction" that brought about the marriage and to delusion "partly due to a trap laid for him by Dunstan, who saw in his brother's degrading marriage the means of gratifying at once his jealous hate and his cupidity" (ch. 3). Godfrey has been set up for blackmail, and the blackmailer is more hateful than his victim. Though George Eliot is severe with both—in marked contrast with her sympathy for Marner—Dunstan's sneering and general nastiness at least make Godfrey's weakness tolerable. But then she carefully brings the two story-lines together, and this relatively shallow blackmail plot makes its contribution to the first of the multiplot novels. Though *Silas Marner* is a short work and is sometimes called a "fable," it has this important position in George Eliot's canon. As Fred C. Thomson has argued, the double plot and theme of discontinuity henceforth become her principal means of testing the relation of individuals to society.[5] (...)

Godfrey can take out his feelings on his brother Dunstan, and so can the reader. By this means the character, the novelist, and the reader are able to "get over" a past life and repair a personal identity.

This process would be more apposite if Godfrey had a career, which he has not—all he really needs to save him is the death of his first wife, so that he can marry again. It is noteworthy that subsequent victims of blackmail in the works of George Eliot do have careers, and not in confectionery either, but in such fields as politics, banking, and mercenary marriage. In the other plot of *Silas Marner*, the hero can be said to have a career, though a humble one. Indeed, the point is that Marner has two careers, the first having been destroyed, along with his religious faith, promised marriage, and social life, by the treachery of one William Dane. The latter is not a blackmailer like Dunstan Cass—blackmailers do not destroy their prey—but he is parallel to Dunstan to the degree that the other has set a "trap" for his brother, and the early victimization links Godfrey and Silas Marner together before they are linked as the two fathers of Eppie.[6] It is also true that if Marner had set up shop in Raveloe in some more ambitions style, instead of becoming a recluse, he might have been subject to blackmail because of the circumstances under which he left Lantern Yard. But Marner has taken even his false conviction upon himself, and it has made a deeper alteration in his character than a blackmailer might effect. He has, in fact, a good deal in common with his author: a reputation for cleverness, a kind of knowledge, a loss of faith, removal to another place, a measure of infamy, semiseclusion, increasing capital, and an adopted child. He has not really fallen, has not stolen a penny, and has not opened himself to blackmail as Godfrey Cass has.

Of the characters with discontinuous careers in *Silas Marner*, the author apparently sympathizes with Marner and judges Godfrey. Readers are likely to respond similarly, scarcely realizing how divided this response is. For those tempted to scorn someone who has been unable to make the two halves of his life meet, Godfrey Cass suffices as a target. To yield to this response, however, is curiously to side with the much more despicable Dunstan Cass. One of the uses of a blackmailer in fiction entails this contradiction: the figure is antithetical to the protagonist (both protagonists in this case) and yet functions in some helpful way. Dunstan, perversely enough, is the one who threatens to make Godfrey accountable for his actions; he threatens to tell what ought to be confessed. He is at once more careless of responsibility than his brother and a bad conscience. Dunstan, like David Faux, is a thief as well as a blackmailer; and by stealing Marner's gold, just before Godfrey's child wanders in the door, he assists in the second and healthier change in Marner's life. Still more obligingly, he steps into the stone pit with the gold and drowns. Dunstan has his uses, and when both actions of *Silas Marner* meet, his is the pivotal role.

While reproving Godfrey Cass's behavior as a young man, the narrator launches into a sermon against trusting to chance. "Favourable Chance is the god of all men who follow their own devices instead of obeying a law they believe in." Five examples of "the worship of blessed Chance" are set forth, with elaborate parallel irony, rounded out by a reductio ad absurdum: "The evil principle deprecated in that religion is the orderly sequence by which the seed brings forth a crop after its kind" (ch. 9). What is Dunstan's role in this thicket of irony? Like many blackmailers, including our friends Tracy and Raffles, he personifies the risk inherent in the religion of chance and in all concealment. He is the narrator's cat's-paw, more on the side of the sermon than its object. Yet what is his further role in the action of *Silas Marner*? It is he who gives the lie to the sermon, by creating the principal interruption or violation of "the orderly sequence by which the seed brings forth a crop after its kind" in the novel, the improbable chance that makes possible the fairy-tale transformation of gold coin into a golden child. The chapter that brings Dunstan to the edge of the stone pit (ch. 4) is a model of George Eliot's ability to narrate circumstances, character, and the character's rationalizations in brief compass, but this effective realism scarcely conceals the commitment of the double plot to chance. Dunstan's presence also helps obscure the fact that Godfrey's Salvation—Godfrey, the original hapless idolator of Chance—comes about at this time through the pure chance of the death of his first wife. Dunstan Cass performs so well for George Eliot because he is so eminently expendable, and he is apparently so wicked that he makes good the operation of chance.[7]

NOTES

5. "The Theme of Alienation in *Silas Marner*," *Nineteenth Century Fiction*, 20 (1965), 82–84. Cf. Jerome Thale, *The Novels of George Eliot* (New York: Columbia University Press, 1959), p. 75.

6. David R. Carroll, "*Silas Marner*: Revising the Oracles of Religion," in *Literary Monographs*, ed. Eric Rothstein and Thomas K. Dunseath, vol. I (Madison: University of Wisconsin Press, 1967), pp. 175–181.

7. Something similar might be said of the expendability of Molly Cass. Novelists can be almost routinely cruel, and the coincidence of Molly's death is presumably acceptable because she is a drug addict and meditating "vengeance" (ch. 12). *Silas Marner* is still a fairly early experiment for George Eliot, however; one cannot imagine Mrs. Glasher in *Daniel Deronda* sinking down on the snow, though Mrs. Glasher is both an inconvenience and a blackmailer.

> —Alexander Welsh, *George Eliot and Blackmail*, (Cambridge, Massachusetts: Harvard University Press, 1985): 163–167.

JOHN HOLLOWAY ON RAVELOE AND THE CREATION OF AN EXAMPLE

[John Holloway was Professor of Modern English and a Fellow of Queens' College at Cambridge University for 44 years. He was the author of the memoir *A London Childhood*, and the critical work *Language and Intelligence*. Here he explains how in her creation of Raveloe, George Eliot offers a comprehensive view of the human situation.]

It would, with George Eliot, be therefore a mistake to begin by noticing incidents, metaphors, snatches of conversation, or similar details. What must be given primary stress is the broad outline, the whole movement of her novels as examples of life that claim to be typical. 'How unspeakably superior', wrote Matthew Arnold, 'is the effect of the one moral impression left by a great action treated as a whole, to the effect produced by the most striking single thought or by the happiest image'.[1] This is as true of the work of the sage-novelist as it is of classical drama or the epic poem. To ignore it is to miss the wood for the trees.

Silas Marner, perhaps because it is simple and short, shows this most plainly. It is worth examining in some detail. Silas the weaver, expelled from his little nonconformist community through a trick of blind chance, settles as a lonely bachelor in the obscure Midland village of Raveloe; one son of the local landlord steals his savings but is unsuspected, and Eppie, the daughter of another by a secret marriage, appears as a foundling at his cottage and he adopts her. Many years after, when she is a young woman about to marry, and her father Godfrey is middle-aged and has married again, the truth about her birth and about the robbery comes at last to light. Various things lend the tale its distinctive quality. First, the characters and their doings seem to belong to the same order of things as the non-human world that surrounds them. The little village, off the beaten track in its wooded hollow, is half submerged in the world of nature. The villagers are 'pressed close by primitive wants'.[2] The passage of time and the rotation of the seasons affect humans and animals and plants all alike. Individuals are dominated by their environment. 'Marner's face and figure shrank and bent themselves into a constant mechanical relation to the objects of his life, so that he produced the same sort of impression as a handle or a crooked tube, which has no meaning standing apart'.[3] It follows from this that all the people in the book are humble and obscure; they may be attractive or virtuous, but they are all nobodies. Silas is a poor weaver who finds hard words in the prayer-book, Godfrey Cass is a squireen's son and a barmaid's husband, Eppie marries a gardener—even Nancy Lammeter, Godfrey's second wife, is only a trim farmer's daughter who does the baking and says 'oss'. Such, the tale implies, is the staple of men and women.

The pattern of events in which these people are involved is one of 'poetic justice': vice suffers, virtue is rewarded. Silas, though unfortunate at first, is a good man, and at last is made happy. Godfrey Cass, who refused to acknowledge his daughter, has no children by his second marriage. Dunstan Cass the rake, stealing Silas's money at night, falls into the pond and is drowned. But this justice is rough and partial. It is not vindictively stern, so much as impersonal and aloof and half-known; it takes a slow chance course, and meets human imperfections not with definite vengeance but with a drab pervasive sense of partial failure or limited success. For the peasantry of such places as Raveloe 'pain and mishap present a far wider range of possibilities than gladness and enjoyment'. For Silas in his time of misfortune the world is a strange and hopeless riddle. His money is taken, Eppie arrives, through the operation of forces that he venerates without comprehending. Done injustice by a sudden twist of fate, he comes to trust in the world again over a long period of years, as the imperceptible influence of Eppie gradually revives long-dead memories and emotions; over the same period his estrangement from the other villagers is slowly replaced by intimacy. His life is governed by habit, and so is theirs. We never learn whether his innocence ever became clear to the congregation that expelled him as a thief.

Though the book is so short, its unit of measurement is the generation: Silas young and old, Eppie the child and the bride, Godfrey the gay youth and the saddened, childless husband. The affairs of one generation are not finally settled except in the next, when Silas's happiness is completed by Eppie's marriage, and Godfrey's early transgressions punished by her refusal to become Miss Cass. Dunstan Cass's misdeeds are not even discovered until, twenty years after the robbery, his skeleton is found clutching the money-bags when the pond is drained; and this is brought to light through, of all things, Godfrey's activities as a virtuous, improving landlord. Well may the parish-clerk say 'there's windings i' things as they may carry you to the fur end o' the prayer-book afore you get back to 'em'. All in all, the world of the novel is one which, in its author's own words, 'never *can* be thoroughly joyous'. The unhappiness in it comes when natural generous feelings are atrophied by selfishness: Dunstan steals, Godfrey denies his daughter. And the consequences of sin are never quite obliterated; Godfrey must resign himself to childlessness, though resignation is itself a kind of content. Real happiness comes when numb unfeeling hardness, the state of mind for example of the grief-stricken and disillusioned Silas, slowly thaws to warmer emotions of kindliness and love.

This novel contains, therefore, though in little, a comprehensive vision of human life and the human situation. It does so through its deep and sustained sense of the influence of environment and of continuity between man and the rest of nature, through its selection as characters of ordinary people living drab and unremarkable lives, and through the whole course of its action, working out by imperceptible shifts or unpredictable swings of chance to a solution where virtue is tardily and modestly rewarded, and vice obscurely punished by some dull privation. The details of George Eliot's treatment operate within this broader framework.

NOTES

1. Preface to the 1853 Edition of the poems (reprinted in *Irish Essays*, etc., *Works*, vol. xi, pp. 288–9).

2. SM. 6.

3. SM. 25.

> —John Holloway, *The Victorian Sage: Studies in Argument*, (London: Macmillan & Co., Ltd., 1953): 113–116.

HENRY AUSTER ON THE REDEMPTION OF RAVELOE

> [Henry Auster is Professor of English at the Munk Centre for International Studies at Trinity College, University of Toronto, specializing in the ideas of selfhood in nineteenth and twentieth-century narrative. He is the author of *Local Habitations: Regionalism in the Early Novels of George Eliot*. Here he discusses the low moral tone of Raveloe and how Eliot works to redeem the village and its citizens.]

In *Silas Marner*, the author's and the reader's tolerance for crooked noses, dull wits, and cantankerous dispositions is stretched further than in any of her other novels, and in the end, through a highlighting of the latent and redeeming human instincts for fellowship, love, and purposefulness, the tolerance is turned to sympathy. This movement begins with Silas Marner's intrusion into the village and our consciousness of the positive aspects of the contrast between Lantern Yard and Raveloe; it gathers force in Silas's attachment to Eppie, and rises to a sacramental climax in the wedding at the end, which celebrates the long-delayed integration of the alien weaver into the community as well as the marriage of the foundling who is the instrument of that integration.

But the second plot of the novel also exemplifies a qualified redemption of ordinary and fallible humanity; it, too, is related, perhaps even more directly than the first, to the flaws in the environment. For Silas, ignorant and confused as he is, moves, even in his passion for gold, on a more intense and heroic emotional plane than the villagers; but Godfrey Cass, the protagonist of the subplot, embodies in himself the very failings of the community as well as its potential virtues. Strong, healthy, energetic, and good-hearted, he is also undisciplined and indecisive, directed by impulse rather than informed purposefulness and self-control. "His easy disposition" is a natural foil to Silas's narrow and passionate dedication (whether to the faith that he loses, the gold that is stolen from him, or the child that stumbles into his cottage and responds to his love). Where Silas is miserly and abstemious, Godfrey is wasteful and self-indulgent, where Silas is a recluse, Godfrey, though not a complete rake, is gregarious and dissolute. Yet both begin as social outcasts: the weaver because of his strangeness and the young Squire, in his own mind at least, because of his degrading marriage. Their lives are strangely intertwined, and the prodigality and sin of the one are made not only to recoil against him but also to reward the suffering, the emotional craving and spiritual need, of the other. Godfrey's unacknowledged child becomes Silas Marner's link with society and the means of his salvation; eventually she reconciles both men, in their distinct ways, to the significance of their past lives.[7]

With his good intentions and wavering will, Godfrey Cass is an appropriately fallible figure; his flaws are common human imperfections, and it is on his behalf that George Eliot makes her characteristic plea for understanding and compassion and insists on the moral drama played out in the most obscure lives:

The subtle and varied pains springing from the higher sensibility that accompanies higher culture, are perhaps less pitiable than that dreary absence of impersonal enjoyment and consolation which leaves ruder minds to the perpetual urgent companionship of their own griefs and discontents. The lives of those rural forefathers, whom we are apt to think very prosaic figures—men whose only work was to ride round their land, getting heavier and heavier in their saddles, and who passed the rest of their days in the half-listless gratification of senses dulled by monotony—had a certain pathos in them nevertheless. (Chapter III)

She elaborates this insight, evoking a genuine sympathy for "these flushed and dull-eyed men," whose only hope of visionary excitement, of access to "purity, order, and calm," is precariously dependent on a woman's elevating affection. Before he marries Nancy—when indeed he has no real hope of marrying her—Godfrey wastes his life in what George Eliot now regards as the prevailing routine of country squires, the monotonous alternation between anger and dissipation. His own better instincts, however, preserve him from utter degradation; as she says, he is one of those "whom—thanks to their native human-kindness—even riot could never drive into brutality" (Chapter III). Thus it is the pathos of his position that she stresses when she describes the psychological corruption to which Godfrey, with all his admirable qualities, has made himself susceptible. Her pity and understanding act to soften not his delinquency but our attitude to him, so that we become concerned about his predicament even though it seems squalid:

The yoke a man creates for himself by wrong-doing will breed hate in the kindliest nature; and the good-humoured, affectionate-hearted Godfrey Cass was fast becoming a bitter man, visited by cruel wishes, that seemed to enter, and depart, and enter again, like demons who had found in him a ready-garnished home. (Chapter III)

There are no comparable explicit apologies for the low moral tone of Raveloe, but here also, in spite of the village's glaring imperfections, George Eliot guides the reader's feelings away from disdain and toward sympathy—though never toward the enchanted affection and admiration with which she depicts Hayslope. It is near the end of Part One, with Mrs. Winthrop's first visit to Silas's cottage (Chapter X) and, much more decisively, with the condensed account of the weaver's joyous tribulations with the growing Eppie and his awakening responsiveness to his surroundings, that our feelings about the community begin to alter. The community itself, however, is not different at this stage from what it had been earlier. In Chapter X, for example, when Dolly Winthrop comes to comfort Silas (who, desolate after the loss of his gold, is no longer feared by his neighbors but pitied "as a 'poor mushed creatur'"), the villagers are still described as relaxed in their churchgoing, gluttonous in their celebrations, and petty in their relations with one another. After the requisite Christmas Day service, "the red faces [make] their way through the black biting frost to their own homes, feeling themselves free for the rest of the day to eat, drink, and be merry, and using that Christian freedom without diffidence." And Squire Cass's New Year's Eve dance brings together "all the society of Raveloe and Tarley, whether old acquaintances separated by misunderstandings concerning run-away calves, or acquaintances founded on intermittent condescension."

But at the same time that she continues to mock the loose habits and trivial minds of the villagers, George Eliot also begins to show them in a more flattering light. The crucial indication of the change is the "kindlier feeling" with which his neighbors come to regard the disconsolate weaver. Mr. Macey, crusty, complacent, and self-centered, is one spokesman of the general sentiments after Silas's loss; Mrs. Winthrop is another. Her solicitude, "simple theology," and quaint good sense show that the village mentality is capable of transcending its ordinary level. She is actually called a "good wholesome woman" and she personifies, in her quickness of feeling and readiness to help, the ties of fellowship and communal warmth that the monotony, abrasiveness, and slackness of daily intercourse tend to obscure or wear away:

> ... she was in all respects a woman of scrupulous conscience, so eager for duties that life seemed to offer them too scantily

unless she rose at half-past four ... Yet she had not the vixenish temper which is sometimes supposed to be a necessary condition of such habits: she was a very mild, patient woman, whose nature it was to seek out all the sadder and more serious elements of life, and pasture her mind upon them. (Chapter X)

Although there is something almost compulsive about Mrs. Winthrop's restless good nature—her benevolence seems to wear the protective coloring of eccentricity, a little in the manner of Dickensian "do-gooders" like Mr. Jarndyce—she does help to save Raveloe from complete disgrace in the eyes of the author and reader. If Godfrey Cass has redeeming qualities, so has the village as a whole, and Dolly Winthrop embodies them.

But the emphasis on the congenial aspects of rural life that becomes apparent as the villagers respond to Silas's isolation does not cancel out the earlier ironic presentation of its dreary side. The community remains essentially the same, but the author now provides it with an opportunity to demonstrate its humanity, good will, and potential for genuine sociability, which serve to soften, if not erase, our awareness of its crudeness. The movement to elicit the reader's sympathy for the village becomes conspicuous in Chapter X, gains impetus in Chapter XIV (the penultimate chapter in Part One), and reaches its height in Part Two, where Silas Marner's assimilation is amply demonstrated and connected with his past. It is clear that George Eliot, in spite of her ironic presentation of the flaws of Raveloe, approves of Silas's progressive affiliation with its life. She shows systematically how his participation in social intercourse humanizes him; at the same time, quite naturally and without contradicting her previous characterizations, she brings to light the warmth and friendliness of the residents of the village. As Silas appears in church for the first time and shares "in the observances held sacred by his neighbours," as Eppie creates "fresh and fresh links between his life and the lives from which he had hitherto shrunk," we become aware, together with him, of "the ties and charities that bound together the families of his neighbours" (Chapter XIV).

The interest that the villagers take in Eppie and, through her, in Silas makes them appear much more amicable than they did earlier. And their aroused benevolence, corresponding to Silas's revived attentiveness to his environment, imbues the copious, untidy land with the radiance of human affection:

> Hitherto he had been treated very much as if he had been a useful gnome or brownie—a queer and unaccountable creature, who must necessarily be looked at with wondering curiosity and repulsion ... But now Silas met with open smiling faces and cheerful questioning, as a person whose satisfactions and difficulties could be understood. Everywhere he must sit a little and talk about the child, and words of interest were always ready for him: "Ah, Master Marner, you'll be lucky if she takes the measles soon and easy!" ... Elderly masters and mistresses, seated observantly in large kitchen armchairs, shook their heads over the difficulties attendant on rearing children, felt Eppie's round arms and legs, and pronounced them remarkably firm, and told Silas that, if she turned out well (which, however, there was no telling), it would be a fine thing for him to have a steady lass to do for him when he got helpless ... No child was afraid of approaching Silas when Eppie was near him: there was no repulsion around him now, either for young or old; for the little child had come to link him once more with the whole world. There was love between him and the child that blent them into one, and there was love between the child and the world—from men and women with parental looks and tones, to the red lady-birds and the round pebbles.[8] (Chapter XIV)

It is significant that after this point in the narrative the two social occasions that occur in Part Two stand in striking contrast to the conversation at the Rainbow and the dance at the Red House: both take place around the church, and though the second presently shifts to the Rainbow, the occasion, Eppie's wedding-feast, is still a sacrosanct one. The difference between the group scenes in Part One and Part Two does not signify a change or refinement in the rustic temper, but rather sustains a mood appropriate to the affirmation of social ties and coherence. At the very end there is indeed an apparent acknowledgement of the familiar strain of grossness and pugnacity that persists but is for the moment absorbed by the genial spirit of Silas's triumph:

In the open yard before the Rainbow the party of guests were already assembled, though it was still nearly an hour before the appointed feast-time. But by this means they could not only enjoy the slow advent of their pleasures; they had also ample leisure to talk of Silas Marner's strange history, and arrive by due degrees at the conclusion that he had brought a blessing on himself by acting like a father to a lone motherless child. Even the farrier did not negative this sentiment: on the contrary, he took it up as peculiarly his own, and invited any hardy person present to contradict him. But he met with no contradiction; and all differences among the company were merged in a general agreement with Mr. Snell's sentiment, that when a man had deserved his good luck, it was the part of his neighbours to wish him joy. (Conclusion)

The inconspicuous way in which George Eliot here succeeds—through the guests' reminiscences about Silas's history, their open declaration of the story's moral, and their veiled benediction—in reinforcing the sense of a completed narrative does not dim the echo of the first Rainbow scene and its argumentative nature. The rural character responds to conviviality and ceremony, but its gnarled bluntness is incorrigible.[9]

NOTES

7. The connection between Silas and Godfrey has also been noticed by Robert B. Heilman, in "Return to Raveloe: Thirty-Five Years After," *English Journal*, XLIV (1957), 1–10, and Jerome Thale, in his Introduction to *Silas Marner* (Rinehart Editions, 1962), pp. xv–xvi, xix–xxi. I cannot help feeling that Ian Milner, in the generally perceptive essay already cited, allows his ideological preconceptions to distort the nature of the link between Silas and Godfrey. Believing their relationship to manifest George Eliot's interest in class conflict in the contrast between "folk" and "bourgeois" values, he takes a harsher view of the young squire than the author herself. His language, moreover, seems to me extreme: "Godfrey and Silas are fatal opposites brought into a fatal conjunction. The thematic development of Marner's loss and recovery of his humanity is counterpointed with the stages of Cass's moral deception and defeat" (p. 725). The best treatment of the

relationship between Silas and Godfrey is to be found in David R. Carroll's *"Silas Marner*: Reversing the Oracles of Religion," *Literary Monographs*, ed. Eric Rothstein and Thomas K. Dunseath (Madison, Milwaukee, and London, 1967), I, 165–200—an excellent essay which I read too late to apply to the present work.

8. The passage (especially in its climax and conclusion) resonantly echoes and confirms the epigraph of the book from Wordsworth's "Michael": "... a child, more than all other gifts / That earth can offer to declining man, / Brings hope with it, and forward-looking thoughts..."

9. In his Introduction to the Rinehart Edition, Thale writes that "the portrait of Raveloe life is relatively free of pastoral glamorization. The famous Rainbow scene may suggest community, but it also suggests dullness and bad temper. Silas may gain happiness by his reintegration, but the community which he becomes part of is neither ideal nor idealized" (p. xiii). Milner emphasizes mainly the warmth and vitality of the Raveloe popular community," its "pulsing communal life" (p. 720).

—Henry Auster, *Local Habitations: Regionalism in the Early Novels of George Eliot*, (Cambridge, Massachusetts: Harvard University Press, 1970): 188–194.

PLOT SUMMARY OF

Middlemarch

Middlemarch appeared slowly—laterally as well as sequentially
—in eight parts. Its views of failed marriages and unrealized
dreams and its characters' fallibilities prompted some critics to
deem it too morbid and serious for its time. Still, *Middlemarch*
was the novel that turned Eliot into an icon. Her complex study
of disorder in a seemingly ordered provincial society—
questioning, among other institutions the clergy, the electoral
process, and the medical profession—prompted Virginia Woolf,
in 1925, to say that "with all its imperfections [it] is one of the
few English novels written for grown-up people."

The novel opens upon two orphan women of marriageable
age. The striking eldest, Dorothea Brooke, is determined to live
an ascetic life and gives the bulk of her mother's jewelry
collection to her younger sister, Celia. Sir James Chettam comes
to dinner with their bachelor uncle, Mr. Brooke, and discusses
Dorothea's plans for public housing; even after he suggests
enacting them on his estate, Dorothea is far more interested in
speaking with Mr. Casaubon, a clergyman whom she thinks
possesses a "great soul." Though Sir James wishes to marry her,
Mr. Brooke summons Dorothea and tells her Casaubon has
asked for her hand. Excited by the prospect of helping Casaubon
with his work, she accepts. Exploring Casaubon's estate,
Dorothea and Celia meet Will Ladislaw, the grandson of
Casaubon's estranged aunt. At her engagement party, Dorothea
meets Tertius Lydgate, a new Middlemarch doctor intent on
discovering the unifying tissue of life. Rosamond Vincy and her
brother Fred, children of the mayor of Middlemarch, visit their
elderly uncle, Peter Featherstone, who accuses Fred of
accumulating debts under the assumption of a large inheritance.
When Fred protests, Featherstone insists he procure a letter
from the banker, Mr. Bulstrode, declaring his innocence. Fred is
in love with Mary Garth, Featherstone's caretaker and niece
through a previous marriage.

Bulstrode hopes to name Lydgate the head of the new fever hospital and insists on Mr. Tyke as its chaplain, instead of Featherstone. Mr. Vincy's preference is also for Tyke—Lydgate remains impartial. Bulstrode tells Mr. Vincy he disapproves of Fred's habits, but finally agrees to write Fred's letter for Featherstone. Upon receiving it, Featherstone offers Fred a hundred pounds as a gift. Even so, Fred is still in debt to Mr. Bambridge, a neighborhood horse dealer.

In Rome, Dorothea is afflicted by unspeakable sadness— Casaubon is cagey and distant and soon the newlyweds are quarreling. Ladislaw's painter friend, Naumann, notices her in a gallery and persuades her to sit for a portrait. One day, Ladislaw goes to visit the Casaubons but only Dorothea is home. When Casaubon returns, he is cold and disapproving of their conversation.

Fred approaches Caleb Garth, who co-signs his debt. He then loses money on a lame horse and forces the Garths deeper into poverty. Fred falls ill and when the Vincy's doctor, Mr. Wrench, is unavailable, Lydgate diagnoses him with typhoid fever.

When the Casaubons return from Rome, Celia reveals that she is engaged to Sir James Chettam. Casaubon takes ill and Lydgate recommends that the scholar work less. Later, Dorothea finally reads a letter from Ladislaw that says he is on his way to England. Mr. Brooke writes to Ladislaw, saying that if he is not to be received at Lowick, he should visit Tipton Grange.

Rumors abound that Rosamond and Lydgate are secretly engaged. Mrs. Bulstrode confronts Rosamond, who denies the claim, and warns her that Lydgate is not a wealthy man. The gossip is heard by Lydgate, who vows to stay away from Rosamond. Soon, though, Featherstone's grave illness draws Lydgate to Stone Court, and when he encounters a distraught Rosamond, he wishes to comfort her and soon finds himself engaged. Mr. Vincy disapproves of the match.

One night, Featherstone tells Mary Garth that he's written two wills and commands her to help him burn one. Worried of the consequences, Mary refuses to make the change, and Featherstone dies in the night, clasping a heap of gold. After the funeral, Featherstone's lawyer, Mr. Standish, reads both wills. The second, prevailing will leaves nothing to Fred and almost the entire fortune to Featherstone's illegitimate son, Joshua Rigg.

Brooke has taken on Ladislaw as the editor of his liberal newspaper, *The Pioneer*, and expresses a desire to run for Parliament. Ladislaw, who has decided to stay in Middlemarch, visits the Casuabons; disapproving of Casaubon's treatment of Dorothea, he vows to watch over her. Dorothea suggests to Casaubon that he leave half of his wealth to Ladislaw to make up for his family's estrangement of Ladislaw's grandmother for marrying a Polish man. Casaubon, without telling his wife, writes Ladislaw and forbids him to come to Lowick again.

A rival newspaper has accused Brooke of hypocrisy, since he trumpets liberal causes but lets his own tenants live in squalor. Dorothea urges her uncle to practice what he preaches. Even so, he approaches one of his tenants, Dagley, about rebuking his son for poaching. Dagley says he'll do nothing of the sort and informs Brooke that all of Middlemarch is speaking of his hypocrisy.

Sir James asks Caleb Garth to manage both his estate and Brooke's. Vicar Farebrother arrives at the Garths' saying that Fred, back at school, has asked him to try and convince his father to let him pursue another occupation. Garth also reveals that Bulstrode wishes to buy Stone Court from Joshua Rigg Featherstone. Meanwhile, Joshua Rigg Featherstone argues with his greedy stepfather, John Raffles. Rigg Featherstone insists he will pay Raffles an allowance and no more. Angry, Raffles notices a letter from Bulstrode and pockets it.

Casaubon's health and marriage is under strain. When Dorothea goes to visit Lydgate, he reassures her that Casaubon could live for fifteen years. They discuss the politics of fundraising, and Lydgate says Bulstrode's unpopularity is the reason for their bad luck. Middlemarch reaction to Lydgate's practice and politics is mixed—many are suspicious of unconventional methods. Bulstrode gives Lydgate chief control over the patients in the hospital, and out of protest, the other town doctors refuse to visit it. Rosamond tells her husband that she wishes he wasn't involved in medicine.

Most of Middlemarch shares Casaubon's disapproval of Ladislaw. Smitten by Dorothea, he goes to Lowick Church to catch a glimpse of her. Later that night, Casaubon asks Dorothea to make a promise. When she asks what it is, he demurs, and in the morning, he takes a walk. While he's gone, Dorothea resolves to do whatever her husband might wish. She finds him seated on a bench and discovers that he's dead.

After Casaubon is buried, Dorothea is embittered to learn he's added a codicil to his will revoking her inheritance if she marries Ladislaw. Unaware of the codicil, Ladislaw wonders why he's being encouraged to stay away from Tipton Grange. After giving an election speech where he notices an effigy of himself in the crowd, Brooke informs Ladislaw that he's been fired because he is selling *The Pioneer*. Upon Lydgate's recommendation, Farebrother is granted Lowick Parish. He plans to court Mary Garth, but when Fred asks him to speak to her on his behalf, he does so. Mary says that she won't marry Fred if he becomes a clergyman, but when Farebrother hints at his own feelings for her, she says she loves Fred too much to forsake him.

Raffles interrupts a conversation between Caleb Garth and Bulstrode. Raffles learns that Bulstrode has purchased Stone Court and Bulstrode bribes Raffles to stay away from him. Raffles has the power to ruin Bulstrode's reputation because he prevented his first wife from finding her daughter and her daughter's child, Ladislaw.

Dorothea returns to Lowick, and Ladislaw visits her with news that he's leaving town. Dorothea hires Caleb Garth to manage Lowick and Garth negotiates the controversial construction of a railroad through the parish. Fred Vincy stumbles on an argument between Garth and some railway agents and when Garth's assistant is wounded in the struggle, Fred lends a hand. He confesses his love for Mary and asks Garth if he might serve him, since Mary will not marry him if he joins the clergy. Though his wife had expressed disapproval, Garth agrees to instruct him; the Vincy's are disdainful of the news, saying their son has thrown away his upbringing. Fred visits Mrs. Garth, who says that Mary's love for him surprised her and that Fred made a mistake in asking Farebrother for help. Fred is surprised and threatened by the news that Farebrother also loves Mary, and he thinks he has no chance.

Lydgate's cousin, Captain Lydgate, comes to visit, and against Lydgate's advice, twice takes Rosamond riding; the second time, she suffers a miscarriage. When Lydgate reveals they are in debt, he refuses Rosamond's suggestion to ask her father for advice. Lydgate mentions the codicil to Rosamond, but forbids his wife from telling Will; Rosamond defies her husband.

Bulstrode hires Ladislaw to attend an auction on his wife's behalf. There, he meets Raffles, who says he knew Ladislaw's mother and that her parents made their fortune from stolen goods. Raffles meets Bulstrode and continues to blackmail him. Bulstrode confronts Ladislaw, confessing that he married Ladislaw's grandmother, saying he was unable to find her daughter—Ladislaw's mother—and offers him an inheritance, which Ladislaw denies because Dorothea wouldn't approve. Mrs. Cadwallader gossips that Will is still in Middlemarch and has designs on Rosamond. Dorothea remembers seeing them together, and when she confronts Ladislaw about the reasons for his lingering, he says what he cares for most is forbidden and that he must go. Distraught that Dorothea doesn't beg him to stay, Ladislaw leaves the next day.

Lydgate tells Rosamond that they must move into a cheaper house and says he hopes to negotiate a deal with Ned Plymdale, Rosamond's former suitor. Rosamond begs her husband to write to his uncle, Sir Godwin, for help, but Lydgate refuses. Rosamond secretly revokes Lydgate's offer on the Plymdale house and writes to Sir Godwin herself. She finally confesses to meddling in the sale, and soon after, a letter arrives from Sir Godwin rebuking him for having his wife meddle in his affairs. Though he is angry with Rosamond, her hysterics cause him to back down.

Bulstrode needs medical attention and Lydgate says he seems to be under a great deal of stress. Bulstrode says he's considering withdrawing support of the hospital and leaving Middlemarch. He says Lydgate should approach Dorothea about supporting the hospital. When Lydgate asks him for a loan, Bulstrode refuses and says the doctor should declare bankruptcy. An ill-looking Raffles arrives at Bulstrode's on Christmas Eve; the next morning he's sent away with 100 pounds. Bulstrode asks Caleb Garth to manage Stone Court in his absence, and Garth considers giving the job to Fred. Soon, Garth comes to the bank and says he's spoken to Raffles and is therefore unable to do business with Bulstrode. Lydgate meets Bulstrode at Stone Court and diagnoses Raffles with the effects of alcoholism. Bulstrode gives Lydgate a thousand pounds; after he leaves, he ceases to follow Lydgate's advice and Raffles dies in the night.

During a town sanitation meeting, the town's condemnation of Bulstrode, and Lydgate, by association, comes to light— Raffles has told the story to a few people. Dorothea learns of Lydgate's plight from Farebrother and insists the doctor cannot be at fault. When Lydgate and Mr. Bulstrode return from the meeting together, Mrs. Bulstrode becomes suspicious—her brother, Mr. Vincy, tells her the entire story. Their confrontation is a tearful one, but they resolve to stay together.

A distraught Rosamond implores Ladislaw to visit. Dorothea approaches Lydgate about making donations to the hospital, but Lydgate says that he must respect Rosamond's wishes to leave town. Dorothea, with a check for a thousand pounds, finds a tearful Rosamond in the arms of Ladislaw. Realizing what Dorothea must think, Ladislaw shakes off Rosamond and rebukes her, but Dorothea is already gone. Later, Rosamond collapses into Lydgate's arms. When Ladislaw returns, Lydgate says Rosamond is ill and tells Ladislaw the story of Raffles.

Dorothea concedes to see Rosamond again and offers to take over Lydgate's debt to Bulstrode. Rosamond later tells Ladislaw that when she spoke to Dorothea, she cleared his name. Ladislaw tells Dorothea that he's refused to take his inheritance from Bulstrode and that he's the grandson of a Jewish thief. Dorothea says that she doesn't care for her inheritance and can survive on her meager income. They become engaged.

Bulstrode remembers that Caleb Garth wanted Fred to manage Stone Court and offers him the job. Fred and Mary marry and live happily with three sons. Lydgate sets up a practice outside of Middlemarch but is never fulfilled—he dies at age 50. Rosamond is constantly jealous of Dorothea; after Lydgate dies she marries a wealthy physician. Ladislaw becomes involved in public reforms and Dorothea is happy being a wife and a mother—their son inherits Mr. Brooke's estate.

LIST OF CHARACTERS IN

Middlemarch

The protagonist of the novel, **Dorothea Brooke** longs to improve the world and draws plans to improve the cottages on larger estates. She lives with her sister and her bachelor uncle, Mr. Brooke. Believing Casaubon to be a great intellectual, she marries him but later discovers that he is not passionate. After he dies, she defies her late husband's wishes and marries his cousin, Will Ladislaw. She helps Lydgate after his problems with Bulstrode.

The bachelor uncle of Dorothea and Celia, **Arthur Brooke** lives at Tipton Grange. Although he lets his own tenants live in poverty, he runs for a seat in Parliament on the Reform platform. He hires Will Ladislaw to write for his liberal paper, *The Pioneer*, and when his political plans fail, he fires him.

Dorothea's sister, **Celia Brooke** is more preoccupied with wealth and material possessions than her older sister. She marries Sir James Chettam.

No one knows the origins of **Nicholas Bulstrode**, a wealthy banker who arrived in Middlemarch 20 years earlier. He earned respectability by marrying Walter Vincy's sister and says he's a deeply religious Evangelical Protestant. But his past is a dark one—he made is fortune selling stolen goods. He married Will Ladislaw's grandmother after her husband died and her daughter had run away. When she insisted Bulstrode find her daughter, Bulstrode hired Raffles—when Raffles found them, Bulstrode never said anything. He buys Stone Court from Joshua Rigg Featherstone.

Harriet Bulstrode is Walter Vincy's sister, and Bulstrode's wife. When she learns of Bulstrode's deception she is upset, but eventually agrees to stand by her husband.

Elinor Cadwallader is the meddling wife of Humphrey, the rector of Tipton Grange. She attempts to arrange a marriage between Dorothea and Sir James Chettam, and when that fails, she pairs Celia with Chettam. After Casaubon's death, she attempts again to make a match for Dorothea.

A scholar whose lifelong ambition is to write a Key to All Mythologies, **Edward Casaubon** is insecure about his capabilities and unfeeling to his wife, Dorothea. He offers financial support to Will Ladislaw (Casaubon's aunt was disowned by the family for marrying a man they didn't approve of and running away) but is envious of Ladislaw's relationship with Dorothea.

A baronet who owns large estate called Freshett, **Sir James Chettam** enacts Dorothea's cottage plans on his estate. Though he initially wishes to marry Dorothea, he marries her younger sister, Celia, instead.

Mr. Dagley is Brooke's impoverished tenant who accuses him of hypocrisy. Though his son is caught poaching on Brooke's grounds, he refuses to rebuke him.

The vicar **Camden Farebrother** gambles to make ends meet and to pursue his scientific hobbies. He befriends Lydgate. He loses the election for the chaplaincy at the New Hospital but receives Lowick parish after Casaubon's death. Though he is in love with Mary Garth, he helps Fred Vincy court her.

The wealthy widower who owns Stone Court, **Peter Featherstone** married twice but has no children. His first wife was Caleb Garth's sister and his second wife was Lucy Vincy's sister. He says he'll leave his fortune to Fred Vincy, his nephew by his second marriage, but he leaves his fortune to his illegitimate son, Joshua Rigg.

Caleb Garth has a large heart but a poor head for business. He manages large Middlemarch estates and eventually takes over Lowick upon Casaubon's death. Against his wife's advice, he co-signs a debt for Fred Vincy, who later loses the money. He declines to manage Stone Court after the revelation of Bulstrode's dark past.

Caleb Garth's daughter and Featherstone's niece by his first marriage, **Mary Garth** works as caretaker for Featherstone. She has simple needs and strong convictions—when, as a result of Fred Vincy, her family falls deep into debt, she works tirelessly. Suspicious of the hypocrisy of the clergy, she refuses to marry Fred if he becomes a vicar.

Will Ladislaw is the grandson of Casaubon's disinherited aunt. He falls in love with Dorothea and is forbidden from seeing her by his cousin. He doesn't care for money or material wealth and wishes only to work for Reform causes.

The orphan son of a military man, **Tertius Lydgate** chooses to be a doctor despite the objections from his wealthy relatives. He hopes to find the tissue that is the basic building block of life. His first love was an actress who killed her husband onstage. He hoped to put off marriage but quickly becomes engaged to Rosamond Vincy before he knows it.

Naumann is Ladislaw's painter friend in Rome who is taken with Dorothea's beauty. As a ploy to paint her portrait, he asks Casaubon to sit as a model for Thomas Aquinas.

John Raffles is bribed by Bulstrode to keep existence of the daughter and grandchild of his first wife secret, and he later blackmails him—when he becomes ill, Bulstrode cares for him but purposely ignores the advice of Lydgate, which causes his death. He is Joshua Rigg Featherstone's stepfather.

Peter Featherstone's illegitimate son **Joshua Rigg** inherits Stone Court and then sells it to Bulstrode so he can be a moneychanger.

The Evangelical minister supported by Bulstrode, **Walter Tyke** wins the election to be chaplain at the New Hospital.

Walter Vincy is the mayor of Middlemarch and modestly well off. He refuses to lend Lydgate and Rosamond money and disapproves of his son Fred's apparent laziness. He is also the brother of Harriet Bulstrode.

Lucy Vincy is the sister of Peter Featherstone's first wife and the daughter of an innkeeper; she dotes on Fred and believes that his work and marriage to Mary Garth are beneath his class.

Rosamond Vincy is the daughter of Walter and Lucy Vincy who wishes for a life of comfort and fine things. Intrigued by Lydgate's apparent noble background, she marries him. But when the doctor falls into debt, she attempts to seek the comfort of Will Ladislaw.

The eldest son of Walter and Lucy Vincy, **Fred Vincy** is sent to college to be a clergyman. He gets into debt by gambling and ends up betraying the Garth family, although he is in love with their daughter, Mary.

Mr. Wrench is the Middlemarch doctor who misdiagnoses Fred's fever. When Lydgate diagnoses Fred correctly Wrench is fired by the Vincys.

CRITICAL VIEWS ON
Middlemarch

LESLIE STEPHEN ON SAINT THERESA

[Leslie Stephen was a nineteenth-century British philosopher and scholar; he was the first editor of the *Dictionary of National Biography*. In addition to biographies of Johnson (1878), Pope (1880), Swift (1882), George Eliot (1902), and Hobbes (1904)—all written for the "English Men of Letters" series—he is also author of *History of English Thought in the Eighteenth Century*, *The English Utilitarians*, and the *Science of Ethics*. Here he discusses the role of Saint Theresa in Middlemarch.]

"Middlemarch" is undoubtedly a powerful book, but to many readers it is a rather painful book, and it can hardly be called a charming book to anyone. The light of common day has most unmistakably superseded the indescribable glow which illuminated the earlier writings.

The change, so far as we need consider it, is sufficiently indicated by one circumstance. The "prelude" invites us to remember Saint Theresa. Her passionate nature, we are told, demanded a consecration of life to some object of unselfish devotion. She found it in the reform of a religious order. But there are many modern Theresas who, with equally noble aspirations, can find no worthy object for their energies. They have found "no coherent social faith and order," no sufficient guidance for their ardent souls. And thus we have now and then a Saint Theresa, "foundress of nothing, whose loving heart-beats and sobs after an unattained goodness tremble off and are dispersed among hindrances instead of centring in some long recognisable deed." This, then, is the keynote of "Middlemarch." We are to have one more variation on the theme already treated in various form; and Dorothea Brooke is to be the Saint Theresa with lofty aspirations to pass through a searching ordeal, and, if she fails in outward results, yet to win additional nobility from failure. And yet, if this be the design, it almost seems as if the book were intended for elaborate irony. Dorothea starts with some admirable, though not very novel, aspirations of the social kind with a desire to improve drainage and provide better cottages for the poor. She meets a consummate pedant, who is piteously ridiculed for his petty and hidebound intellect, and immediately takes him to be her hero and guide to lofty endeavour. She fancies, as we are told, that her spiritual difficulties will be solved by the help of a little Latin and Greek. "Perhaps even Hebrew might be necessary—at least the alphabet and a few roots—in order to arrive at the core of things and judge soundly on the social duties of the Christian." She marries Mr. Casaubon, and of course is speedily undeceived. But, curiously enough, the process of enlightenment seems to be very partial. Her faith in her husband receives its death-blow as soon as she finds out—not that he is a wretched pedant, but that he is a pedant of the wrong kind. Will Ladislaw points out to her that Mr. Casaubon is throwing away his labour because he does not know German, and is therefore only abreast of poor old Jacob Bryant in the last century, instead of being a worthy contemporary of Professor Max Müller. Surely Dorothea's error is almost as deep as ever. Casaubon is a wretched being because he has neither heart nor brains—not because his reading has been confined to the wrong set of books. Surely a man may be a prig and a pedant, though he is familiar with the very last researches of German professors. The latest theories about comparative mythology may be familiar to a man with a soul comparable only to a dry pea in a bladder. If Casaubon had been all that Dorothea fancied, if his knowledge had been thoroughly up to the mark, we should still have pitied her for her not knowing the difference between a man and a stick. Unluckily, she never seems to find out that in this stupendous blunder, and not in the pardonable ignorance as to the true value of his literary labours, is the real source of her misfortune. In fact, she hardly seems to grow wiser even at the end; for when poor Casaubon is as dead as his writings, she takes up with a young gentleman who appears to have some good feeling, but is conspicuously unworthy of the affections of a Saint Theresa. Had "Middlemarch" been intended for a cutting satire upon the aspirations of young ladies who wish to learn Latin and Greek when they ought to be nursing babies and supporting hospitals, these developments of affairs would have been in perfect congruity with the design. As it is, we are left with the feeling that aspirations of this kind scarcely deserve a better fate than they meet, and that Dorothea was all the better for getting the romantic aspirations out of her head. Have not the commonplace people the best of the argument? (...)

[I]n "Middlemarch" we feel more decidedly that high aspirations are doubtful qualifications; that the ambitious young devotee of science has to compound with the quarrelling world, and the brilliant young Dorothea to submit to a decided clipping of her wings. Is it worth while to have a lofty nature in such surroundings? The very bitterness with which the triumph of the lower characters is set forth seems to betray a kind of misgiving. And it is the presence of this feeling, as well as the absence of the old picturesque scenery, that gives a tone of melancholy to the later books. Some readers are disposed to sneer, and to look upon the heroes and heroines as male and female prigs, who are ridiculous if they persist and contemptible when they fail. Others are disposed to infer that the philosophy which they represent is radically unsatisfactory. And some may say that, after all, the picture is true, however sad, and that, in all ages, people who try to lift their heads above the crowd must lay their account with martyrdom and be content to be uncomfortable. The moral, accepted by George Eliot herself, is indicated at the end of "Middlemarch." A new Theresa, she tells us, will not have the old opportunity any more than a new Antigone would "spend heroic piety in daring all for the sake of a brother's funeral; the medium in which these ardent deeds took shape is for ever gone." There will be many Dorotheas, and some of them doomed to worse sacrifices than the Dorothea of "Middlemarch," and we must be content to think that her influence spent itself through many invisible channels, but was not the less potent because unseen.

Perhaps that is not a very satisfactory conclusion. I cannot here ask why it should not have been more satisfactory. We must admit that there is something rather depressing in the thought of these anonymous Dorotheas feeling about vaguely for some worthy outlet of their energies, taking up with a man of science and discovering him to be an effete pedant, wishing ardently to reform the world, but quite unable to specify the steps to be taken, and condescending to put up with a very commonplace life in a vague hope that somehow or other they will do some good. Undoubtedly we must admit that, wherever the fault lies, our Theresas have some difficulty in fully manifesting their excellence. But with all their faults, we feel that they embody the imperfect influence of a nature so lofty in its sentiment, so wide in its sympathies, and so keen in its perceptions, that we may wait long before it will be adequately replaced. The imperfections belong in great measure to a time of vast revolutions in thought which produce artistic discords as well as philosophic anarchy. Lower minds escape the difficulty because they are lower; and even to be fully sensitive to the deepest searchings of heart of the time is to possess a high claim on our respect. At lowest, however we may differ from George Eliot's teaching on many points, we feel her to be one who, in the midst of great perplexities, has brought great intellectual powers to setting before us a lofty moral ideal, and, in spite of manifest shortcomings, has shown certain aspects of a vanishing social phase with a power and delicacy unsurpassed in her own sphere.

—Leslie Stephen, "George Eliot," *Discussions of George Eliot*, ed. Richard Stang, (Boston: D.C. Heath and Company, 1960): 21–24.

DAVID LODGE ON NARRATION AND THE "CLASSIC REALIST TEXT"

[The British novelist and critic David Lodge has taught at the University of Birmingham, during which time he wrote studies of Graham Greene and Evelyn Waugh. His works of criticism include *The Language of Fiction* and *Modes of Modern Writing*, and his latest work of fiction, *Thinks*, was published in 2001. Here he disagrees with post-structuralist critic Colin McCabe's contention that *Middlemarch* is a "classic realist text" that represents experience concretely through language. The example he uses is a discussion of Camden Farebrother.]

Now it is true that the narrator's discourse in George Eliot's fiction is modelled on the I–thou speech situation, and certain that she would have endorsed Wordsworth's description of the writer as a man speaking to men. But in obvious ways, whether consciously or unconsciously, she reminds us that her narration is in fact written. This is particularly true of the more ostentatiously diegetic passages, when she suspends the story to deliver herself of opinions, generalizations, judgements. To call these passages transparent windows on reality, as MacCabe does, seems quite inappropriate. They are in fact often quite obscure, or at least very complicated, and have to be scrutinized several times before we can confidently construe their meaning—a process that is peculiar to reading, and cannot be applied to the spoken word. Consider, for example, this comment on Mr Farebrother, shortly after Lydgate has voted against him in the selection of the hospital chaplaincy.

> But Mr Farebrother met him with the same friendliness as before. The character of the publican and sinner is not always practically incompatible with that of the modern Pharisee, for the majority of us scarcely see more distinctly the faultiness of our own conduct than the faultiness of our own arguments, or the dullness of our own jokes. But the Vicar of St Botolph's had certainly escaped the slightest tincture of the Pharisee, and by dint of admitting to himself that he was too much as other men were, he had become remarkably unlike them in this that he could excuse others for thinking slightly of him, and could judge impartially of their conduct even when it told against him.

I would defy anyone to take in the exact sense of this passage through the ear alone. There are too many distinctions being juggled, and too many swerves and loops in the movement of the argument: first, we encounter the idea (stated in a double negative, and thus made more difficult to assimilate) that the modern publican and sinner may be combined with the modern Pharisee in the same person, unlike their Biblical prototypes. Is Mr Farebrother, who has just been mentioned, such a person, we may wonder, as we begin to negotiate this passage? This would be inconsistent with the previous presentation of his character, but we have to wait for some time to be reassured that this is not what the narrator means. Before we come to that point, we have to wrestle with another distinction—between faults of manners (arguments and jokes) and faults of morals (conduct)—a distinction which doesn't correspond exactly to the one between publicans and sinners and Pharisees. The exculpation of Farebrother is highly paradoxical: by admitting that he is too much like other men, he becomes remarkably unlike them: which is to say, that by admitting he is a publican and a sinner, he avoids being a Pharisee as well. So why has the narrator introduced the concept of Pharisee at all? It seems to be floating free, and we puzzle our way through the paragraph, waiting to see to whom it applies. We may be disconcerted to realize that it is applied, explicitly, only to 'the majority of us' ourselves. Perhaps it is also applied implicitly to Lydgate, whose conduct over the election, as he himself is well aware, was not entirely disinterested. On reflection we may decide that the negative comparison between Farebrother and Pharisee is justified by the fact that the Pharisees were a Jewish religious sect and that Phariseeism is an occupational failing of men of religion, but this explanation scarcely leaps off the page.

Mr Farebrother seems to emerge from these complex comparisons with credit. But only a few lines later, after a speech from Mr Farebrother in direct (i.e. mimetic) form—

'The world has been too strong for me, I know', he said one day to Lydgate. 'But then I am not a mighty man—I shall never be a man of renown. The choice of Hercules is a pretty fable; but Prodicus makes it easy work for the hero, as if the first resolves were enough. Another story says that he came to hold the distaff, and at last wore the Nessus shirt. I suppose one good resolve might keep a man right if everybody else's resolve helped him.'

—we encounter this diegetic comment:

The Vicar's talk was not always inspiriting: he had escaped being a Pharisee, but he had not escaped that low estimate of possibilities which we rather hastily arrive at as an inference from our own failure.

This seems to check any inclination on the reader's part to overestimate Mr Farebrother's moral stature; and if, in reading the preceding diegetic passage, we mentally defend ourselves against the accusation of Phariseeism by identifying ourselves with Farebrother's candid admission of his faults, we now find ourselves implicated with him in another kind of failing—complacency about one's faults. But if we make another adjustment, and take this as a cue to condemn Farebrother, we may be surprised and disconcerted once more, to find ourselves identified with Lydgate—for the passage immediately continues, and ends (as does the whole chapter) with this sentence: 'Lydgate felt that there was a pitiable lack of will in Mr Farebrother.' Since Lydgate has just been portrayed as subordinating his own will to expediency in the matter of the chaplaincy election, he is hardly in a position to throw stones at this particular moral glasshouse, and the sequel will show even greater 'infirmity of will' on his part in the matter of Rosamond. To sum up, the authorial commentary, so far from telling the reader what to think, or putting him in a position of dominance in relation to the discourse of the characters, constantly forces him to think for himself, and constantly implicates him in the moral judgements being formulated.

—David Lodge, "Middlemarch and the Idea of the Classic Realist Text," *George Eliot*, ed. K.M. Newton, (New York: Longman Group, 1991): 179–181.

RICHARD FREADMAN ON CHARACTERIZATION, FROM LYDGATE TO RAFFLES

[Richard Freadman is Professor of English in the La Trobe University English program. He is the author of *Renegotiating Ethics in Literature, Philosophy, and Theory* and *Rethinking Theory: A Critique of Contemporary Literary*

Theory and an Alternative Account. Here he examines Eliot's methods and motives for characterization in *Middlemarch*, from the painstakingly drawn Lydgate to the almost caricature-like Raffles.]

Middlemarch's pastoral creations are given in extraordinary detail. As John Bayley notes, the classic example is Lydgate, who is introduced in Chapter 15. This chapter, which was to have been the beginning of a separate narrative, offers the most extensive background description in the novel: his childhood, his discovery of a vocation, his intemperate romantic experience—all are adduced with high explanatory seriousness. So, too, is a more elusive feature of his temperament, the famous 'spots of commonness' (I. 15, p. 228) that are to betray an in many ways admirable and sophisticated man into fatally flawed and derivative life choices. These 'spots' appear to represent not quite temperament *per se*, but rather the way in which a vulnerable personality may absorb the tragically inadequate codes—romantic, professional and other—that betray so many characters in both George Eliot and James. In all of this the portrait of Lydgate has the virtues and failings of the self-evident. The narrator selects and interprets with that high sobriety that often marks Eliot's least suggestive mode of character creation:

> For those who want to be acquainted with Lydgate it will be good to know what was that case of impetuous folly, for it may stand as an example of the fitful swerving of passion to which he was prone, together with the chivalrous kindness which helped to make him morally lovable. (Ibid.)

To 'stand as an example'—that is very much the import of this character, though, as we shall see, the 'delicate crystal' (III. 64, p. 181) that is his marriage elicits some of the novel's most sensitive insights into knowledge and relationships.

At the other end of the narrative spectrum is such a character as Raffles, that refugee from the world of Dickensian caricature. Raffles has none of the poignant appeal of Eliotean inwardness. Like Grandcourt, he is a kind of ontological exile from the world of moral agency and as such does not elicit the customary range of solicitous interest and compassion. If many of George Eliot's creations are 'characters of love', Raffles, as his introduction illustrates, is emphatically a character of hate:

> He was a man obviously on the way towards sixty, very florid and hairy, with much grey in his bushy whiskers and thick curly hair, a stoutish body which showed to disadvantage the somewhat worn joinings of his clothes, and the air of a swaggerer, who would aim at being noticeable even at a show of fireworks, regarding his own remarks on any other person's performance as likely to be more interesting than the performance itself. (II. 41, pp. 212–13)

That Raffles is at this stage little more than 'a cluster of signs' does not in this instance discourage the narrator from categorical judgment. The 'air of a swaggerer' suffices to fix the inner man and it is noticeable how quickly and uncritically the description modulates from physical notation to a kind of accusatory psychological shorthand about unregenerate egoism (Raffles's fixation on his 'own remarks' rather than their subjects). As Lydgate reflects the metonymic inclusiveness of the Eliotean method, so Raffles is a creature of metaphor, an exile from the redemptive anxiousness of narrative attention. Yet he is, by virtue of this, oddly opaque and memorable. Raffles springs complete from authorial indignation, and, if we feel that George Eliot has here given us nothing to esteem, there is also a suspicion that much about such a man eludes even her powers of insight. A margin of self is as it were unintentionally implied: the withdrawal of sympathy infuses this, the most derivative portrait in the novel, with a special status. In *Bleak House* Raffles would be less than incidental. Here he is quite disproportionately prominent. Like Bulstrode, the narrator can 'get no grasp over the wretched man's mind' (III. 69, p. 253), and the rogue's awfulness transcends the expository convenience of his entanglement in the plot.

—Richard Freadman, *Eliot, James and the Fictional Self: A Study in Character and Narration*, (New York: St. Martin's Press, 1986): 144–145.

SANDRA M. GILBERT AND SUSAN GUBAR ON IMAGES OF
ENTRAPMENT

[Sandra M. Gilbert is Professor of English at University
of California, Davis and Susan Gubar is Distinguished
Professor of English at Indiana University. They co-
authored *The Madwoman in the Attic: The Woman Writer
and the Nineteenth-Century Literary Imagination* and the
Norton Anthology of Literature by Women, for which they
received a *Ms.* Women of the Year award. Their most
recent works are a collection of poetry for and about
mothers, *MotherSongs*, and a satire on the current state of
literacy and cultural literacy, *Masterpiece Theatre: An
Academic Melodrama*. Here they discuss how Dorothea is
imprisoned not just by Casaubon, but by many of
Middlemarch's male characters; they also explain how
Rosamond is a foil for Dorothea.]

At the beginning of *Middlemarch* Dorothea is searching for the
keys not only to her mother's casket of jewels, the beauty of
which promises revelations, but also for the way out of a "walled-
in maze" of prospective identities as Mrs. Cadwallader's future
Lady Chettam, the narrator's Saint Theresa, or a self-defined
architect for the poor. Like Maggie Tulliver, who wanted "some
key that would enable her to understand," Dorothea associates
this key "with real learning and wisdom, such as great men
knew," (*MF*, IV, chap. 3), so she chooses the role of Milton's
daughter. But she quickly realizes that Casaubon will be unable
to provide her with the learning and wisdom she had hoped to
gain. In spite of her frustration and disappointment, Dorothea
discovers that it is easier "to quell emotion than to incur the
consequences of venting it" (chap. 29), so she begins to see as
intelligible images of "saints with architectural models in their
hands, or knives accidentally wedged in their skulls," whereas
before such figures had always seemed monstrous (chap. 20).
    Nevertheless, although Dorothea searches for "something
better than anger and despondency" (chap. 21), throughout her
married life with Casaubon, even in her humility, she causes him

pain, even robbing him of the illusion of professional dignity with her urging that he actually begin to write the book he has so studiously planned. These words are "among the most cutting and irritating to him that she could have been impelled to use" (chap. 20). To Casaubon she is "a spy watching everything with a malign power of inference" (chap. 20), and he correctly judges her silences as "suppressed rebellion" (chap. 42). Her outward compliancy masks her indignation, superiority, and scorn; when expressed, these feelings result in Casaubon's collapse on the library steps; "the agitation caused by her anger might have helped to bring on" the attack of illness (chap. 30). When Dorothea's identification with Aunt Julia brings her to question the economic basis of patriarchy, specifically Casaubon's right to determine his own will and fix the line of succession in spite of his past familial obligations, she causes the most damage. Angry yet terrified about the murderous potential of her emotion, she is "wretched—with a dumb inward cry for help to bear this nightmare of a life in which every energy was arrested by dread" (chap. 37). Her marriage becomes "a perpetual struggle of energy with fear" (chap. 39). When Casaubon rejects the pity she expresses upon discovering that he suffers from the (metaphorically perfect) "degeneration of the heart," Dorothea is "in the reaction of a rebellious anger" (chap. 42). "In such a crisis as this," we are told by the narrator, "some women begin to hate" (chap. 42).

Dorothea's physical and emotional situation is similar to Maggie Tulliver's:

> Somehow, when she sat at the window with her book, [Maggie's] eyes would fix themselves blankly on the outdoor sunshine; then they would fill with fears, and sometimes ... she rebelled against her lot, she fainted under its loneliness; and fits even of anger and hatred ... would flow out over her affections and conscience like a lava stream, and frighten her with a sense that it was not difficult for her to become a demon. [MF, IV, chap. 3].

Dorothea's strong need to struggle against "the warm flood" of her feelings (chap. 20) is proof of the strength of her rebellion, and she finds in repression "the thankfulness that might well up in us if we had narrowly escaped hurting a lamed creature" (chap. 42). But, again like Maggie Tulliver, she realizes that "we have no master-key" for the "shifting relations between passion and duty" (*MF*, VII, chap. 2). Deciding to resign herself to the life-in-death scenario Casaubon constructs for her, Dorothea bends to "a new yoke" in the belief that she is "going to say 'Yes' to her own doom" (chap. 48); however, her hesitation through the night before acquiescing fully in Casaubon's stipulation that she dedicate herself to his research after his death implicates her in that death, at least in her own mind. (...)

But it is with Rosamond that we must associate Eliot's most important study of female rebellion. The Lilith to Dorothea's Mary, Rosamond is associated early in the novel with sirens, serpents, and devilishly alluring charms. She entangles Lydgate into courtship and then covertly rebels against his mastery, harboring secret designs and willfully asserting her right to enjoy herself. Because Rosamond threatens her father to go into a decline if she cannot have her own way, because her wilful persistence in going horseback riding during her pregnancy against her husband's orders causes her to miscarry, most critics considered her an example of that egoism which Eliot condemns as narcissistic, and certainly we might be tempted to accept Lydgate's view of her as a kind of Madame Laure who would kill him because he wearied her, while we define Dorothea as another sort of woman altogether (chap. 56). But we have already seen that Dorothea is involved in a "form of feminine impassibility" that Rosamond more overtly typifies (chap. 56). Both, moreover, are called angels, each achieving her own perfect standard of a perfect lady, and both are considered beautiful. Both are victims of a miseducation causing them not to "know Homer from slang" (chap. 11), and neither, therefore, shows "any unbecoming knowledge" (chap. 27). Experiencing the frustrating truth of Mrs. Cadwallader's remark, "A woman's choice usually means taking the only man she can get" (chap. 54), Dorothea and Rosamond can only express their dissatisfaction with provincial life by choosing suitors who seem to be possible means of escaping confinement and ennui.

For both, then, marriage is soon associated "with feelings of disappointment" (chap. 64). Oppressed by the gentlewoman's "liberty" (chap. 28), both are resentful that their husbands perceive them only as graceful yet irrelevant accoutrements and both presumptuously attempt to recreate their respective husbands in their own images. Like Dorothea, Rosamond feels that her girlish dreams of felicity are quickly deflated by the inflexible reality of intimacy and while both women struggle to repress their resentment, both find some consolation in the visits of Will. Indeed, when his visits cease, both find themselves looking wearily out the windows of their husbands' houses, oppressed by boredom. Dorothea in Lowick and Rosamond in Lowick Gate try to ease their loneliness in part by writing to their husbands' relatives.

As their common marriage struggles suggest, these women are tied to men who increasingly resemble each other, not only in their careers but in their conjugal lives. When Rosamond expresses her opinion about debts that will affect her life as much as his, Lydgate echoes Casaubon: "You must learn to take my judgment on questions you don't understand" (chap. 58). Lydgate contemptuously calls Rosamond "dear," as Casaubon does Dorothea when he is most annoyed with her presumption. The narrator expresses sympathy for Lydgate's need to bow under "the yoke," but then goes on to explain that he does this "like a creature who had talons" (chap. 58). Lydgate begins to act and speak "with that excited narrow consciousness which reminds one of an animal with fierce eyes and retractile claws" (chap. 66). Like Casaubon, Lydgate will "shrink into unconquerable reticence" (chap. 63) out of personal pride when help is offered. And like Casaubon he experiences the discontent "of wasted energy and a degrading preoccupation" (chap. 64). Fallen into a "swamp" of debt (chap. 58), he feels his life as a mistake "at work in him like a recognized chronic disease, mingling its uneasy importunities with every prospect, and enfeebling every thought" (chap. 58).

Lydgate had dreamed of Rosamond as "that perfect piece of womanhood who would reverence her husband's mind after the fashion of an accomplished mermaid, using her comb and looking-glass and singing her song for the relaxation of his adored wisdom alone" (chap. 58)—a dream not appreciably different from Casaubon's. But this suitor whose distinction of mind "did not penetrate his feeling and judgment about furniture, or women" (chap. 15)—as if these are interchangeable goods—ends up in a losing struggle with his wife about furniture. Admitting that he has gotten an inexperienced girl into trouble (chap. 58), he knows that "she married [him] without knowing what she was going into, and it might have been better for her if she had not" (chap. 76). Lydgate attacks Rosamond's attachment to their house, thinking "in his bitterness, what can a woman care about so much as house and furniture" (chap. 64), but she has been given nothing else to care about. She "could not have imagined" during her courtship that she would "take a house in Bride Street, where the rooms are like cages" (chap. 64).

Having no overt means of escape at her disposal and a husband who refuses to hear or take her advice, Rosamond enacts her opposition as silently as does Dorothea; she is "particularly forcible by means of that mild persistence which, as we know, enables a white living substance to make its way in spite of opposing rock" (chap. 36). Always able to frustrate him by stratagem, Rosamond becomes Lydgate's basil plant, "flourishing wonderfully on a murdered man's brains" (Finale).

—Sandra M. Gilbert and Susan Gubar, *The Madwoman in the Attic: The Woman Writer and the Nineteenth-Century Imagination*, (New Haven: Yale University Press, 1979): 510–512; 514–516.

D.A. MILLER ON PERSPECTIVE AND DOROTHEA AT THE WINDOW

[D.A. Miller is a Professor of English and Comparative Literature at Columbia University. He is the author of *Narrative and Its Discontents: Problems of Closure in the Traditional Novel, Bringing Out Roland Barthes* and *The Novel and the Police.* Here, analyzing a late scene where Dorothea, distraught, looks out her window, Miller discusses perspective from the character's point of view as well as the narrator's.]

Dorothea's spiritual crisis contains the concentrated experience of what being in a narrative means in *Middlemarch*. 'The limit of resistance was reached, and she had sunk back helpless within the clutch of inescapable anguish' (p. 844). Will's presumed defection to Rosamond has been a betrayal of 'the vibrating bond of mutual speech' (p. 844), and Dorothea's own utterances can barely get further than 'loud-whispered cries and moans' and 'helpless sobs' (p. 845). The 'detected illusion' of Will's 'lip-born words' closes every prospect but that of an endless, pointless narrative (p. 845). In a sense, Will's loyalty to her stood as a bulwark against the dispersive influences of time and change: it offered a 'sweet dim perspective of hope, that along some pathway they should meet with unchanged recognition and take up the backward years as a yesterday' (p. 844). With that hope gone, Dorothea's life threatens to be kept forever in a state of unresolved, unresolvable transition.

Her response to this threat—the narrative threat *par excellence*—comes with violent, all but masochistic intensity. She locks herself in her 'vacant room', as though to underscore the void of her solitude; she presses 'her hands hard on top of her head', as though delivering again the psychic wound inflicted by Will; she lies 'on the bare floor and let[s] the night grow cold around her', as though this were the only appropriate metaphor for her state of mind (p. 844). One might argue that her dramatic gestures are already part of an effort to master the anxiety they repeat. For they stress her despair in a double sense: they emphasize it, *and* they put pressure on it to give way. Dorothea's acting out—what the narrator calls her 'paroxysm' (p. 845)— seems unconsciously organized by the expectation that, if she can only intensify her concentrated experience even further, she may finally provoke 'the ultimate act which ends an intermediate struggle'. To raise the fever might be to break it in the end; to cultivate nightmares might be at last to wake up from them. Compared by the narrator to 'a despairing child', Dorothea unwittingly pursues the logic of tantrum, inflating itself in order to subside.

Her impatience, so to speak, is rewarded: 'She had waked to a new condition: she felt as if her soul had been liberated from its terrible conflict; she was no longer wrestling with her grief, but could sit down with it as a lasting companion and make it a sharer in her thoughts' (p. 845). Once more Dorothea struggles to assert a vision in which 'everyday-things mean the greatest things', though this time with a crucial difference. In the past, we noticed, Dorothea's commitment to the signified took place at the expense of an attention to the signifier. Vehicles were overlooked or dismissed altogether by a peremptory tenor, which then found nothing to carry it. Suggestively, Dorothea's grief can now yield to a less disabling vision precisely through a new interest in detail *together with* a speculation about meanings. 'She began now to live through that yesterday morning again, forcing herself to dwell on every detail and its possible meaning.' What is generally identified as Dorothea's emancipation from ego involves, specifically, a dual challenge: to inspect the details overlooked by a repressively selective selfhood, and to consider the meanings these might have for *others*. In the light of the polycentric perspective Dorothea tries to achieve ('Was she alone in that scene. Was it her event only?'), the range of the world's details and the range of meanings that can be made available to them need no longer restrict one another. If one meaning only reductively grasps a scene, then another meaning—or a whole range of other meanings—may be more adequate to the task. And yet, if meaning may be finally adequate to scene, is scene adequate to meaning? Can scenes fully incarnate the meanings that grasp them? The view from the window would seem decisive in its affirmation:

> She opened her curtains, and looked out towards the bit of road that lay in view, with fields beyond, outside the entrance-gates. On the road there was a man with a bundle on his back and a woman carrying her baby; in the field she could see figures moving—perhaps the shepherd with his dog. Far off in the bending sky was the pearly light; and she felt the largeness of the world and the manifold wakings of men to labour and endurance. She was a part of that involuntary, palpitating life, and could neither look out on it from her luxurious shelter as a mere spectator, nor hide her eyes in selfish complaining. (p. 846)

Meaningfulness and life are in this moment reconciled, immanently charged with one another. As Martin Price has seen, 'the sublimity [Dorothea] has sought in heroic exertions of the ego gives way to a sublimity she finds at a new level of her own being as well as of the world's'.[7] Under the pressure of Dorothea's insight, this tiny diorama of the everyday emblematically extends and insinuates itself beyond its borders so that it comes to implicate, virtually, the entire world. And the world, which before had been seen as irrelevantly petty, now encompasses all that there is to live for. Together with the vision that sees it so, it can sustain the largest and most ambitious meanings available to it.

Yet—one says it almost with regret—even this scene invites us to question its adequacy to the meanings it is supposed to be at last fully representing. What Dorothea sees from the window is inevitably qualified by the text's showing of what she doesn't see. I don't simply mean the fact that the tentativeness of certain details ('*perhaps* the shepherd with his dog') implicitly refers us to her notorious shortsightedness (p. 53), although this does suggest that her capacity to *feel* 'the largeness of the world' depends partly on a physiological inability to *see* it. Her more telling lapse of vision involves passing over the social dimension of the landscape, along with the social conditions of her own observation. Dorothea is the owner of an estate: her view opens out from a window on it and passes directly through its 'entrance-gates'. The fields beyond may well be part of the property. Significantly, Dorothea never sees anyone she knows in this landscape; she never even sees anyone she could know. No male protagonist of *Middlemarch* would ever be seen laboring in the fields, nor would Celia or Rosamond ever appear on the road carrying her baby. The horizontal view across the landscape masks the vertical view downward to a different class. At the moment of Dorothea's greatest participation in 'that involuntary, palpitating life', she is removed from it by obvious social divisions. During her most democratic vision, she is *looking down*, both literally and in terms of social hierarchy. In a sense, the same oversight that permits her to identify with those she sees ironically brings the validity of identification into question.

Moreover, if Dorothea unwittingly censors the scene by not reading its social codes, the resulting picture of the human condition in turn censors her problems by not admitting them into its space. For life seen from the window is stripped to its most essential imperatives: survival (hence work) and procreation (hence 'child-bearing'). The synecdoche whereby Dorothea makes these imperatives stand for her own less elementary dilemmas has its obvious therapeutic uses, but it also leaves out a lot. To the figures in the landscape, of course, physical labor and child-bearing have an immediate and unquestioned relevance. Dorothea's situation, however, is precisely one in which work and womanhood have become *problems*. Both her income and her good faith have made it possible to embark on a quest determined neither by economic necessity nor by traditional social arrangements. In this light, the symbolic equations of the vision ('burden' equals production equals 'man', 'baby' equals reproduction equals 'woman') either make that quest irrelevant or are made irrelevant by it. Once again, the solution seems below the level of the problem, and the answer comes to a question we thought was very different.

Furthermore, the answer isn't all there. Much as in the Bulstrodes' reconciliation, its plenitude is both promised and postponed. The scene has only given voice to 'an approaching murmur that would soon gather distinctness' (p. 847): its full truth will come later. The deferment inevitably detotalizes the scene's glimpse of transcendence, as though it were always a receding vision needing to be filled in, even when it was taking place. Paradoxically, the seemingly all-inclusive moment *lacks something*: its meaning can have the status of an ultimate truth only if it is carried through, supplemented, translated. In other words, the scene commits its closural status to the very processes that define the narratable. The vision thus risks being lost in the effort to find itself. Even before considering the first consequence of that effort (Dorothea's 'second attempt to see and save Rosamond'), one should recognize the insistent disjunction between this scene and that. How is Dorothea to transfer the basic and grand values announced in the view from the window to the sophisticated and petty issue of Rosamond's adulterous temptation? The largeness of Dorothea's vision seems already impugned by the smallness—or simply the otherness—of the first opportunity to carry it through. Since the vision has deferred its meaning until more explicit and specific revelations to follow, much might ride on the visit to Rosamond: no less than the possibility of answering the question, Has Dorothea's vision taken place? ...

In every case, then, what the great scenes of *Middlemarch* aspire to signify is exceeded by their signifiers, which just as easily point to blindness, misunderstanding, egocentric tautology, and textuality, as they do to insight, recognition, fellowship, and transparency. It is as if the novelist could not help seeing the persistence of the narratable even in its closure. As a consequence, closure appears to take place only through a strategic misreading of the data—a misreading that is at once shown to be expedient (expressing a moral command), efficacious (settling the final living arrangements of characters), and erroneous (deconstructed as a repetition of what it is supposed to overcome). The resulting ambiguity, of course, is bound to make conclusion less conclusive. George Eliot herself recognized that 'conclusions are the weak point of most authors, but some of the fault lies in the very nature of a conclusion, which is at best a negation'.[8] Or as we might say: the suspensive and dispersive logic of narrative is such that an effective closure—no matter how naturally or organically it emerges from the story—always stands in a discontinuous (or negative) relation to it.

NOTES

7. MARTIN PRICE, 'The Sublime Poet: Pictures and Powers', *Yale Review* 58 (Winter 1969), p. 213.

8. *George Eliot Letters*, ed. Gordon S. Haight (New Haven: Yale University Press, 1954–55), 2, p. 324. My attention was brought to the letter in question by Darrel Mansell, Jr, 'George Eliot's Conception of "Form"', *Studies in English Literature* 5 (Autumn 1965), pp. 651–62, reprinted in George R. Creeger, *George Eliot: A Collection of Critical Essays* (Englewood Cliffs, N.J.: Prentice-Hall, 1970), pp. 66–78. In an excellent study, Mansell argues that 'the more relations the novel establishes, the more must be severed where they do not end ... at best the conclusion can only cut off this network at some arbitrary point' (p. 77). My only quarrel with Mansell's theory of form in George Eliot (which he bases on the novelist's own essay, 'Notes on Form in Art') is

that his interest in the 'relations which the novel itself sends outwards' leads him to scant the extent to which a novel like *Middlemarch* tries to master its internal dynamic in quasi-conventional resolutions.

> —D.A. Miller, "George Eliot: The Wisdom of Balancing Claims," *George Eliot*, ed. K.M. Newton, (New York: Longman Group, 1991): 193–197.

Robert Coles on Bulstrode, the Most Powerfully Drawn Character

[Robert Coles is a research psychiatrist for the Harvard University Health Services, Professor of Psychiatry and Medical Humanities at Harvard Medical School, and James Agee Professor of Social Ethics at Harvard University. His books include *Children of Crisis*, for which he won the Pulitzer Prize, and over sixty works on psychology, literary criticism, and teaching. He is also the editor of *Double-Take* magazine. Here he traces the evolution of Nicolas Bulstrode and explains how he is Eliot's most richly complex character.]

In certain respects Bulstrode is the most powerfully drawn character in *Middlemarch*—the strongest person, the one we struggle with most, perhaps the one from whom we learn the most. Even in the prelude we are told that Dorothea will never quite live up to her possibilities. Dr. Lydgate wins our admiration; later on he disappoints us, or we cover up our impatience toward him with pity. Ladislaw is indeed weakly portrayed; if only he *were* a first-class dilettante—anything to give some direction to his personality. Casaubon is not so easily dismissed, thanks to the author's stubborn sympathy for everyone she creates. But an old, tired man obsessed with obscure philosophical points is hardly the one to capture our imagination. He, too, becomes pitiable—and maybe at times defended by us as an object of exploitation: it is no joy to become an instrument of an another's moral passion. In contrast, Bulstrode seems to appear out of nowhere and ultimately vanish with no trace left—yet he is unforgettable, even haunting.

He is a banker at first acquaintance, a newcomer to

Middlemarch, one who is selfish, and again, power-hungry, but also progressive. The old established wealth, such as that possessed by Dorothea's brother-in-law Sir James Chettam, is unobtrusive and arguably more dangerous. Sir James wants no changes. Why should a perfectly ordered and comfortable Middlemarch be undone by new ideas, new programs? He is the staunch conservative, not romanticized, however. He has his clear interests, and will fight to defend them. He is haughty, smug, self-satisfied—and headed for a decline in power as a result of the political reforms on the brink of being enacted. Celia loves him and he is good to her, provided she keep within the limits he has set. His antagonism to Dorothea is maintained throughout the novel—he had first wanted to marry her—and only somewhat attenuated, in a live-and-let-live arrangement at the very end; for such stubborn pique we are disposed against him. He uses social custom to enforce his whims and prejudices. But his manners and background shield him from criticisms Bulstrode easily comes upon.

Sir James manipulates, pulls levers of influence, dominates, inflicts vengeance—but all the while displays impeccable manners. As a result he is seen as a proper gentleman. Refinement cloaks a mind's nature, a person's deeds. Bulstrode has no such sanctuary. He is blunt and forceful, looked up to because he is a man of means, but not for any other reason. No one in Middlemarch at that time wanted to lose its aristocrats; and one way of keeping them is to be blind to their schemes and warts, their solid capacity to be as malevolent as anyone else. Bulstrode was always there, a man to be feared and suspected. He may have done many things to warrant just such an attitude from his fellow Middlemarchers, but even before the critical drama of his life unfolds, we find him no mere greedy banker. His bluntness and candor contrast with the deceit that social prominence can cover up. His reformer's instincts are also apparent. He is a rational man, and impatient with outmoded traditions, or superstitions. He is with Lydgate in his desire to reform the medical profession. True, his progressive inclinations are with justice seen as excuses for his greed or ambition. If the old customs are ended, the old authorities weakened, his kind of aggressive wealth has a much easier time extending itself.

But reform was needed badly, and George Eliot makes it all

too clear that the kind of enlightened, regenerative conservatism Edmund Burke placed his faith in was simply not forthcoming in Middlemarch. Sir James Chettam is no political monster, anxious to turn the clock back and keep everyone firmly under tow. He is quite simply self-contented without exception. He will lift no finger to make anyone else even remotely as well-off as he is. Consequently, others have to have the nerve, the drive, the skill and cunning, to move in, if not take over. Then it is, of course, that the Chettams of this world look surprised: why the uproar? And besides, look at those complaining or trying to exert their influence—their gall, their coarseness! Meanwhile, not a few people, whatever their actual needs, side with the Chettams. Perhaps they are people who have given up hope for any change in their own condition—or perhaps they find satisfaction in favoring what is established and has an aura of respectability and gentility, as against the brash, the new, the somewhat ungraceful. Perhaps, not unlike Hobbes or Edmund Burke, they prefer the authority that is, and dread the uncertainty if not the chaos which often enough accompanies social change.

There are rhythms to injustice which become familiar; new noises, however promising, only grate upon the ears. Nor is resignation of a highly philosophical kind to be dismissed as beyond the ken of a peasant. Caleb Garth, who abruptly turns on Bulstrode, is more than a peasant, anyway, though he has the somewhat exaggerated honor and righteousness city people in search of heroes sometimes grant peasants. They are felt to be so good, those men of the earth—so decent, so hard working, so uncorrupted, so near to being Rousseau's natural man. They are credited with seeing so much—more than the Bulstrodes, more than the Chettams, more than the Casaubons, even the Lydgates—and also with being beyond temptation: they hold everything together. However, the truth may simply be they stand with the prevailing system often enough, and block social and political changes that might well help them live better. They do so not out of virtue, nor out of malice, either. They do not wish to cut their noses to spite their faces. Resignation may indeed be the word. They feel in their bones what the new programs and leaders will bring: yet more mischief.

Against such a background of forces and counter forces,

established authority and rising power, crying needs and grave doubts about anyone's reasons for meeting those needs, Bulstrode suddenly moves from a peripheral figure, one of those minor Middlemarchers who have mainly sociological interest for us, into the exact center of the novel's stage. With him comes Raffles, whose name and manner are right out of Dickens. With him, too, comes an acceleration of drama that almost takes the reader aback. After nearly five hundred pages of almost stately progression (which reflects England's remarkable nineteenth-century capacity for gradual but significant political transformation) we suddenly meet up with blackmail, night-terrors, political anguish, a virtual murder, followed by the swift exposure and ruin of a prominent citizen.

All this is done, however, with a minimum of melodrama. Even more important, the author shirks other temptations. She has already told us how pious a man Bulstrode is, how devoted to evangelical religion. She might easily have exposed not only him but his beliefs—his constant outward show of "faith," his larger corruptions of spirit which more than match the lies and deceptions Raffles happens to have known and threatens to reveal. A pompous banker who preaches Jesus Christ's message, then goes on to the next bit of cynical, financial double-dealing, Bulstrode may not be the first hypocrite in the history of the novel, but one might have thought him irresistible to George Eliot. She has never been really cruel to any of her characters, but she is a teacher and a moralist, and Bulstrode offers her the resort to a serviceable tradition of edifying satire.

Properly restrained, yet deftly used, such satire can be enormously suggestive. The world is full of show and pretense, and we crave their unmasking. Particularly helpful is the novelist who doesn't ruin the job with scorn; then we become uncomfortable because we feel somehow cheated. Insincerity and sanctimony are not as flagrant and extraordinary as some satirists make them out to be. Anyway, we fancy ourselves sophisticated, and we want a subtle if not gentle analysis; that way a lot more ground can be covered, many more connections made. After all, Bulstrode was not Middlemarch's only liar or crook dressed up in good clothes and married well and able to intimidate people not only financially but morally. Pharisees plagued Christ; and this side of heaven they persist everywhere—certainly in churches all over that bear His name. He was betrayed by His disciple; He is betrayed every day by those who call on others to believe in Him. It is an old story, and Middlemarch is no special place where a different twist to the story will be found. Or so it seems for a while, as Raffles wields his power and Bulstrode begins to crumble—though he fights back with every resource at his command.

Yet, gradually the author introduces a new element in her narrative. She reveals how skilled a story-teller she can be; as mentioned, the narrative quickens, and plenty of action takes place. But more than that happens. At a certain point we begin to lose Bulstrode as the object of scorn. We even begin to sympathize with him, however obvious his crimes. Indeed, as he plots and calculates, tries everything his mind, well versed in tricks and bluff, can come up with, we almost wish him success. Raffles is a no-good, and not in any way explored psychologically, so good-riddance to him is easy. But the way Bulstrode's mind is revealed to us contrasts with the level and range of analysis given every other character in the novel. The motives of others are brought to light in a leisurely fashion, and to a great extent, in order to build up a variety of individuals, each of them different in a number of respects. In the case of Bulstrode something else is done. His complexity of character, his anguish, his malevolence, all of it virtually explodes upon us, and before we know it we are strangely caught up—implicated is perhaps the word. The crucial turn in the narrative occurs in chapter 68:

> For Bulstrode shrunk from a direct lie with an intensity dis-proportionate to the number of his more direct misdeeds. But many of these misdeeds were like the subtle muscular move-ments which are not taken account of in the consciousness, though they bring about the end that we fix our mind on and desire. And it is only what we are vividly conscious of that we can vividly imagine to be seen by Omniscience.

We already know that Bulstrode is quite able to deceive people, yet the author now brings up this distinction of "a direct lie." Furthermore, words like "consciousness" and "conscious" appear. Even God becomes Omniscience. The question of awareness gets linked to that of "a direct lie" or "more indirect misdeeds." Bulstrode may not only fool others; it is quite possible that he himself does not know exactly what his intentions are, what he is aiming at, trying to accomplish. We know for sure that this man is no vague, wondering, self-deluded failure. Nor is he a mental case. He seems all too effective and directed in manner. More than others in Middlemarch he seems to have a clear idea of what he is after. Yet, of all things his mind's activity is called into question—almost as if he were alive today and some of our lawyers and psychiatrists, concerned about the issue of right-versus-wrong in the light of psychoanalytic determinism, were not quite sure how to regard the man. To some extent Raffles' behavior, steadily worse, makes us move closer to Bulstrode. Raffles is appeased, bought off, then reneges and makes new demands and threats. He also begins to deteriorate, break his part of the bargain, drink to excess, and talk the same way. And soon he is very sick, quite possibly on his death bed. It is natural for us to feel that Bulstrode may deserve our contempt, but not the injury an alcoholic confidence man and ne'er-do-well wants to impose.

While all that is going on in our minds, George Eliot is moving closer and closer toward Bulstrode's private mental life. His "nervous energy" under the strain is mentioned. There is a marvelous scene in which one kind of liar confronts another. Bulstrode mobilizes his "cold, resolute bearing" and Raffles, so full of swagger, so convinced he has the upper hand, melts. Bulstrode's servants imagine Raffles "a poor relation," rather a nice moment for Bulstrode, given what he is afraid of. And by this time we are enough with Bulstrode to settle for that as a proper punishment: let Raffles properly embarrass him. That way the banker will come off his high horse, and stop preaching all the time. He will have to attend his own before he finds fault with others.

But matters go from bad to worse. Raffles becomes more garrulous, hence dangerous. He also starts becoming a victim of his success. Ever greedy, he demands more from Bulstrode, then drinks away what he has secured. For "various motives" Bulstrode stiffens his defenses, squarely threatens to call Raffle's bluff, but is generous with him, noticing the man's decline and perhaps hoping against hope for more of it. None of that is especially revealing to us, but it is rendered forcefully and tersely. Even when the author comes up with one of her especially pointed paragraphs of a single sentence, ("Who can know how much of his most inward life is made up of the thoughts he believes other men to have about him, until that fabric of opinion is threatened with ruin?") we are still relatively detached from Bulstrode. We have simply been reminded once again that no one's life is all that private; that a society like Middlemarch's works its way into everyone's mind and heart, exacts tributes, prompts attitudes and desires, generates assumptions, imposes restrictions or inhibitions, expects and to a degree obtains a form of allegiance, a code of behavior—all of it, as the rhetorical question indicates, the more influential because submerged in life's everyday flow of feeling and action, rather than noticed and considered.

Relentlessly the author pushes on, however. She goes from those "other men" to Bulstrode. She has this particular person examine himself, wonder why Raffles has come with his threats as well as when he will leave and stay away. "Divine glory" comes to mind: can God have his purposes, unapparent to man? Bulstrode the man of piety had always thought God's purposes could be ascertained—proven visible, even, by a show of religious devotion. Now a more inscrutable and devious God is conjured up by the desperate man. And in such desperation he becomes a deeper, more reflective man. Rather as Adam and Eve must once have, he wonders to himself what God does see: everything? only so much? Anyway, might an apparent disaster be but the advance sign of some good news? Might the Lord visit and chastise those he has singled out for eventual recognition of quite another kind? Is submission to a tormentor like Raffles in truth obedience to God? Or ought one be more self-protective, so that the good Lord sees quite clearly the justice of one's cause, and one's faith in oneself?

As Bulstrode asks himself such questions, directly or by implication, his mind moves back and forth from the things of this world to an almost Biblical resignation before the felt presence of an altogether different World. God's mysterious ways, and Satan's obsess him; and his mental activity does not disintegrate into psychopathology or into cowering religious ingratiation, a last-ditch effort to stave off disaster through Divine intervention. His ruminations and moments of confrontation, not long and not overly dramatic, are nevertheless worthy of St. Augustine's. A sinner, he is also a sincere believer— but also a thoroughly imperfect one. A moral hypocrite and a man capable of being mercilessly out for himself, he can be conscientious, open to new ideas, genuinely self-critical in his own stop-and-go journey toward repentence. He never loses his scheming, vastly materialistic side. He call pray hard and long, while all the time estimating what to do with his various properties. Yet his prayers, his desperate effort to meet with God and understand His purposes, are an unquestionable part of him, and significantly, are not subjected to the author's mockery. Even the obvious irony of his conflicting dispositions begins to wilt under the heat of his scrupulous self-examination before God: we become, with him, totally immersed in a supplicant's religious fervor, and begin to forget his other qualities. In his own way he asks why—not only why Raffles has appeared thus to curse and quite possibly destroy him, but why God tempts man with possibilities, moments of triumph, situations just ambiguous enough to allow the worst to be done in such a way that it seems not so bad, after all, and maybe even, all things considered, rather virtuous.

As Bulstrode struggles with himself, a number of such philosophical and theological issues became subtly absorbed into his moment of intense and prayerful introspection—a psychological "crisis" we would call it. He wonders how God can possibly permit him, a man of avowed faith, to be destroyed by an obvious heathen. He prays, whereas Raffles drinks and has nothing to do with any church. He prays with all his heart and soul, whereas others, his self-righteous creditors, who he fears will soon enough be gossiping about him, go to church on Sundays, but that is that. But if he can't be quite self-righteous himself, he can also feel himself to be in the very midst of a riddle which none of us can ever resolve. "He knew that he ought to say, 'Thy will be done'; and he said it often." On the other hand, he hoped against hope that "the will of God might be the death of that hated man."

—Robert Coles, "Irony in the Mind's Life; Maturity: George Eliot's Middlemarch," *The Critical Response to George Eliot*, ed. Karen L. Pangallo, (Westport, Connecticut: Greenwood Press, 1994): 179–185.

BERT G. HORNBACK ON LADISLAW, DOROTHEA'S UNHAPPY ENDING

[Bert G. Hornback is the President of the Dickens Society. He is Professor of English at Bellarmine University and the author of *Great Expectations: A Novel of Friendship* and the editor of *Bright Unequivocal Eye*. Here he discusses how Eliot's realism is illustrated in her depiction of the fallible Will Ladislaw.]

But as many readers and critics have long said, her reward is only Will Ladislaw—a weak, unworthy, unsatisfactory, and unreal or unrealized creature with a rippling nose and coruscating hair. The key to this criticism seems to be in the term unrealized—and the result of examining what Will is realized as, may be to enable us to see him more positively. By looking carefully at how he is identified and defined in the novel and in relation to the real world upon which the novel is based we can discover why and how he can be Dorothea's reward, and why she has to sacrifice herself a second time—by giving up her future, it seems—to marry him.

One of the most remarkable aspects of *Middlemarch* has been, for many critics, its realism: the way in which the real world is woven together with the fictional. The history of England from 1828 to 1831 is an impressive part of the texture of the novel—so much so that English history and *Middlemarch* seem to be complementary. The medical education and opinions of Lydgate are real, current, and historically reliable. Dorothea's planning, Mr. Brooke's politics, Casaubon's scholarship are all drawn in reference to a real history, as has often been pointed out. But such historical realism is not in itself important to the novel or to the reader's experience of it. This historical, factual dimension becomes a part of the "feeling" that *Middlemarch* produces indirectly upon the reader, as this dimension supports the characters and gives them something like metaphysical validity and authority in their world. Their realization as characters is finally more imaginative than historical, or simply realistic.

Like most of the other characters in *Middlemarch*, Ladislaw is attached to history. Indeed, Will's attachment to historical fact is more direct and personal than that of any other character in the novel. Through this attachment, he is associated with a certain set of aesthetic, imaginative, and philosophic values which, as they are shared with Dorothea, become a kind of morality for George Eliot and provide the novel's resolution. Through these values, as through the other realistic and historical details of the novel, she creates its "feeling," the imaginative experience of the whole.

At the time in history of which she writes, George Eliot says, "Romanticism ... was fermenting still as a distinguishable vigorous enthusiasm in certain long-haired German artists in Rome" (p. 130). Ladislaw's sketching leads him to an association with one of those artists, Adolf Naumann. Joseph Jacobs has thought Naumann's character to be suggested by that of Johann Friedrich Overbeck (1789-1869), the father of the German Nazarene school, who worked in Rome after 1810. Certainly Naumann is representative of that school. He describes Dorothea not so much in the vocabulary of the German Nazarene group as in related English Pre-Raphaelite terms, seeing her as "antique form animated by Christian sentiment—a sort of Christian Antigone—sensuous force controlled by spiritual passion" (p. 132). That is to say, George Eliot is remarking on the past forty years earlier (*Middlemarch* was published in 1871–72, and its action transpires during 1828–31) in the vocabulary familiar to, as well as from the point of view of, a contemporary of the Pre-Raphaelites. Thus, for example, a few pages later she has Will characterize Naumann as "one of the chief renovators of Christian art, one of those who [has] not only revived but expanded that grand conception of supreme events as mysteries" (p. 147)—which is to characterize him as a follower of the Nazarenes. It is not surprising that Will should be defined and situated in these terms, since from about 1850 the Nazarene school had its disciples in England in the Pre-Raphaelites, led in art and in literature by Dante Gabriel Rossetti. Will's interest in painting is influenced by Naumann's work, and he espouses something of the idea of Pre-Raphaelite poetry in saying to Naumann that "Language gives a fuller image [than painting], which [image] is all the better for being vague. After all, the true seeing is within" (p. 133).

Ladislaw's role in *Middlemarch* is in part established by means of this association with Pre-Raphaelitism, as it gives him a set of basic values from which to develop his personal identity. The historical association gives authority—but not necessarily approval—to his character and his way of life. It does not prohibit George Eliot's criticizing him for being a dilettante, though even in that criticism she seems to recognize the measure of his spiritual potential. When he gives up "poetic metres" and "mediaevalism"—which is to say the Pre-Raphaelite affectation—in exchange for the chance of "sympathising warmly with liberty and progress in general" (p. 318), George Eliot comments that "Our sense of duty must often wait for some work which shall take the place of dilettanteism and make us feel that the quality of our action is not a matter of indifference" (pp. 318–19).

Of course Will has never been a petty creature, just a dilettante. His moral point of view is basically similar to Dorothea's—and to Lydgate's. His religion, he says, is "To love what is good and beautiful when I see it" (p. 271). True, by comparison with Dorothea's ambition, to *do* good for other people, Will's sounds—as his creator would have it—somewhat effetely aesthetic, "dilettantish." And adumbrating the decadents of the 1890's, he insists to Dorothea, "I don't feel bound, as you do, to submit to what I don't like" (p. 271). Still, his point of view is important for the novel, and important for Dorothea to understand. Their confrontation in chapter 22 is a significant one. Will tells Dorothea:

> "I fear you are a heretic about art generally. How is that? I should have expected you to be very sensitive to the beautiful everywhere."
> "I suppose I am dull about many things," said Dorothea, simply. "I should like to make life beautiful—I mean every-

body's life. And then all this immense expense of art, that seems somehow to lie outside life and make it no better for the world, pains one...."

"I call that the fanaticism of sympathy," said Will, impetuously. "... The best piety is to enjoy—when you can. You are doing the most then to save the earth as an agreeable planet. And enjoyment radiates. It is of no use to try and take care of all the world; that is being taken care of when you feel delight—in art or in anything else" (pp. 152–53).

Two similar but uncongenial idealisms meet here: the moral ideal, to which Dorothea is devoted, and the aesthetic ideal, by which Will wants to live. In the end they are reconciled by the necessary compromise which makes Will commit himself to work as "an ardent public man" and Dorothea settle for something like the "radiance" of goodness in which Will believes, so that "the effect of her being on those around her was incalculably diffusive" (p. 578).

This ending is not a triumphant one for Dorothea. She still feels "that there was always something better which she might have done" (pp. 575–76), and George Eliot concludes that her marriage to Will was not an "ideally beautiful act, but a sacrifice" (p. 577). And although Dorothea believes (pp. 374–75)—and George Eliot asserts (p. 576)—that Will is no longer a dilettante, he is nevertheless not Hooker, Locke, Milton, or Pascal. He is, however, real and male, a husband for Dorothea and a father for her child. And he is prepared to work in the real world at doing practical things, "working well in those times when reforms were begun with a young hopefulness of immediate good which has been much checked in our days" (p. 576). As for Dorothea, though she is happy in her life with Will, many people, according to George Eliot, "thought it a pity that so substantive and rare a creature should have been absorbed into the life of another, and be known only in a certain circle as a wife and mother. But no one stated exactly what else that was in her power she ought to have done" (p. 576). Despite the resemblances and comparisons, Dorothea is not, after all, St. Theresa, Antigone, the Virgin Mary, or a queen.

Dorothea is only real, not mythical. And in being real, in becoming a woman of responsibility in the real world, she joins the community of Middlemarch. In so doing she proves the vitality and the significance of that community. As the reader looks back now on the "Study of Provincial Life" that he has read, the various characters exhibit a new depth, a new rich dimension of humanity which was not so evident before. There is a "feeling" that "radiates" from Dorothea, affecting one's sense of the whole novel. This happens by means of example and analogue: for not only do the comparative elements in plots and characterization support Dorothea, they are themselves elevated and enhanced by what they share with her.

—Bert G. Hornback, "The Moral Imagination of George Eliot," *The Critical Response to George Eliot*, ed. Karen L. Pangallo, (Westport, Connecticut: Greenwood Press, 1994): 165–167.

GEORGE LEVINE ON ELIOT AND REALISM

[George Levine is Kenneth Burke Professor of English at Rutgers University. He is the author of *Darwin and the Novelists* and *Lifebirds*. In this essay, he discusses how both Eliot and her companion, George Henry Lewes dealt with the mysteries of the universe and how the narrator in *Middlemarch* and Lewes, in his *Problems of Life and Mind* address questions of unreliability.]

Philosophically, Lewes chose to write of the limitations of knowledge with a confidence and clarity that diminished their mystery, but his *Problems of Life and Mind*, like George Eliot's last novels, verges, at times, on the mystical. Certainly, the book implies a world of mystery—if not of the inexplicable, then of the unexplained. Moreover, the world of what Lewes calls "the Invisible," though of dominant importance to human life and psychology, is accessible only to scientific method or to a kind of visionary Intuition (ultimately analyzable to "sensations"). Holding, in the complexity of its myriad relationships, the primary elements of meaning and value, it remains obscure to all but the most passionate (and the passion is a condition for great scientific study) and assiduous investigators. Thus the ordinary world to which George Eliot's realist program was devoted and which would seem to be the center of empiricist epistemology begins to look like a world forever excluded from truth and moral acuity—ultimately, in fact, not even susceptible to direct representation. Although quantity tends to replace the traditional mysteries—"our problem," says John Tyndall, "is not with the quality but with complexity"—there are still mysteries. The citizens of the ordinary world are incapable of understanding it without intuition; and the ordinary, with its organic filaments, is ultimately coextensive with the universe itself. "Every Real," says Lewes, "is the complex of so many relations, a conjuncture of so many events, a synthesis of so many sensations, that to know one Real thoroughly would only be possible through an intuition embracing the universe" (I, pp. 342–43). To penetrate the mysteries of the unknown without surrendering faith in the reality and validity of the material world and the empirical method was the object of both Lewes and George Eliot.

The closest approximation to the sort of intuition necessary for penetrating the mysteries comes, in George Eliot's later novels, in the voice of the narrator which, as we have seen, raises important problems about reliability. But within the novels proper, George Eliot's vision required that she move beyond the world of the "dull grey eyes," since the fullest moral action, dependent on the fullest knowledge, which is itself dependent on the deepest feeling, is available only to the exceptional people in her provincial settings. The moral superiority of the untutored Dorothea Brooke, even over the sensible and educated Mr. Farebrother (who, it turns out, is a bad scientist), derives, for example, from her response to her own deep feelings, her intuitive recognition of "unapparent relations." It is this that leads her to support Lydgate. But Dorothea's moral imagination reflects the other truth—that she is an alien in a world that does not offer itself to common sense, either to Mrs. Cadwallader's or to Celia's. Such people, impelled by feelings issuing only from the experience of "direct relations," act and judge hastily. "There is nothing petty," George Eliot wrote as early as *The Mill on the Floss*, "to a mind that has a large vision of relations." But the question is, how does one achieve such a vision?

The answer, in Dorothea's case and in Lewes's theory, is at

least partially clear: one must be capable of standing outside of oneself (of what might, indeed, be called an ecstasy, so rare and religious in tone does it become). It is to such an ecstasy Dorothea forces herself in the remarkable eightieth chapter of *Middlemarch*. Her immediate feeling of "direct relations"—particularly with Will Ladislaw, whom she has found in a compromised position with Rosamond—has led her for a moment to give up her generous mission to help Rosamond understand Lydgate and to soften the pain of that painful marriage. "How should I act now," she cries almost in prayer near the end of her night's vigil, "if I could clutch my own pain, and compel it to silence, and think of those three?" (p. 577). This familiar and moving sequence in Dorothea's history has its precise analogue in Lewes's evolving theory. It is also coherent with George Eliot's belief in the connection of feeling to knowledge, of knowledge to moral action. In her early review of Mackay's *Progress of the Intellect*, she noted that "we have long experienced that knowledge is profitable; we are beginning to find out that it is moral, and shall at last discover it to be religious."

Dorothea struggles beyond the limits of self by virtue of the power of "feeling," the source, in Lewes's epistemology according to *Problems of Life and Mind*, of all knowledge ("by the Real is meant whatever is given in Feeling" (II, pp. 16–17]). The power of her own feeling allows her to imagine the reality of other people's feeling (Lewes: "by the Ideal is meant what is virtually given, when the process of Inference anticipates and intuites [*sic*] what *will* be or *would* be feeling under the immediate stimulus of the object" [II, p. 17]). We are in the presence here of what we have long recognized as George Eliot's "moral aesthetic," articulated frequently and less "scientifically" in the novels themselves. Obviously, in Lewes's theory and in George Eliot's fiction, the ideal, the making present to self of feelings literally present only to others, is achieved by virtue of the imagination, or, one might say, the power to create workable hypotheses. Only the facts given us by the narrator allow us to verify Dorothea's belief in Lydgate; for Dorothea herself, Lydgate's own explanation is the only evidence. But her hypothesis that Lydgate would not do what the town assumes he has done is a condition for useful action. Imagination seems, in the details of novelistic life, to create reality as much as it "penetrates" it.

But the imagination, in this view, is potentially more real than the observable external fact, the apparent relations; for the imagination can fuse together what the analytic mind has necessarily but arbitrarily separated. For both Lewes and George Eliot, organism was not a metaphor but a fact. Psychology was comprehensible only by bringing together the study of biology, of the organism in which mind is located, and of society, that larger organism—the "medium"—in which the smaller organism of the self exists by virtue of its myriad and complex relations. These conceptions were ultimately verifiable; indeed, the novels test their validity, and (putting aesthetic questions aside) justify themselves as hypotheses are justified—as imaginative constructs essential to the progress of knowledge (hence, of morality), but still only provisionally true. In Lewes's philosophy we find an attempt to construct a large unity of psychology (a discipline avoided by Comte because too focused on the individual) and sociology (the locus of "humanity"). In this construct the self and the other are not two things but one; the objective and subjective are indispensable to each other, are indeed merely different aspects of the same thing. There is no existence without relationship: "Nothing," writes Lewes in *Problems of Life and Mind*,

> exists in itself and for itself; everything in others and for others: *ex-ist-ens*—a standing out relation. Hence the search after *the thing in itself* is chimerical: the thing being a group of relations, it is what these are. Hence the highest form of existence is Altruism, or that moral and intellectual condition which is determined by the fullest consciousness—emotional and cognitive—of relations. [II, pp. 26–27]

George Eliot herself, writing in 1868 her "Notes on Form in Art," reiterates this organicist view: "Forms of art can be called higher or lower only on the same principle as that on which we apply these words to organisms; viz. in proportion to the complexity of the parts bound up into one indissoluble whole."

Complex unity is the ideal, both in art and life. To sustain their tough willingness to acquiesce in the very changes that were fragmenting and desacralizing their worlds, Lewes and George Eliot had to incorporate as richly as possible the complexities which—to common sense—seemed to be shattering the unified vision of an earlier age, and which to Victorian culture as a whole challenged dangerously all the inherited traditions of religion and morality.

But we can see here that for Lewes and George Eliot, unity is transferred from God to organism, an entity that implies continuity and growth, through evolution, interdependence, and therefore self-denial, love, morality, complexity, and mystery. Altruism, a positivist ideal, becomes both a Christian moral imperative and a scientific one.

But here, the impulsion to unity—echoing in the traditional Victorian insistence on self-denial—has the further complication of threatening the very conception of selfhood. The self, in Lewes's view, cannot be understood as a thing in itself, but only as a set of relations. He speaks moreover, elsewhere in *Problems of Life and Mind*, of "mind" as an abstraction that names a process and a set of relationships, not as a stable thing that can explain anything. The self is both "the generalised abstraction of continuous feeling," and a series of "concrete discontinuous states" (II, p. 19). The self, then, is a sum of qualities forever in process. "Character too," says the narrator of *Middlemarch*, "is a process and an unfolding." The notion is put yet more strongly by Clifford. "The universe," he says, "consists of feelings. A certain cable of feelings, linked together in a particular manner, constitutes me. Similar cables constitute you. That is all there is."

As a mere part of an "involuntary, palpitating life," Dorothea's self is almost an illusion and has its value in the larger fate of the species. Although, in accordance with George Eliot's realist aesthetic and her refusal to sacrifice immediate feeling and particularities to ideas, the image that Dorothea sees at the window is particularized, her vision is rapidly assimilated to larger significances. Her moral triumph entails the disappearance of the self and slips back from science to Carlylean self-annihilation. Similarly, the character of the "highest" (i.e., most "altruistic") beings in Eliot's novels is increasingly defined by the absence of what we traditionally think of as character. Where Hardy gives us a "man of character" in Henchard, Eliot gives us Daniel Deronda. That special self-identifying eccentricity, whether Micawber's lamentations or Casaubon's austere defensiveness, is a sign of a demanding self incapable of the necessary absorption in the Lewesian organism.

The austerely theoretic force that lies behind Dorothea's vision is more immediately recognizable in Eliot's poetry, where, as R. H. Hutton early remarked, "the rhythm and music drop a soft cloud over the moral detail of life, and fill her soul with the principles she has generalised from its study, rather than with the minutiae of its scenery." There are no such minutiae at the end of *Jubal*, when the angel comes to console Jubal after his people have failed to recognize him as the godlike founder of music whom they celebrate:

> This was thy lot, to feel, create, bestow.
> And that immeasurable life to know
> From which the fleshy self falls shrivelled, dead,
> A seed primeval that has forests bred.

The grim affirmation here and in *Middlemarch* is too reminiscent of the near despair of Tennyson's famous complaint of Nature: "So careful of the type she seems, so careless of the single life." But in the positivist context, what drives Tennyson to despair constitutes the highest moral affirmation. As Lewes sees the problem in *Problems of Life and Mind*, it is only when one gets beyond the sense of reality available to ordinary perceptions (and thus, also, beyond the conventional sense of character) that one can begin to find the possibility of affirmation.

It is true that our visible Cosmos, our real world of perceptions, is one of various and isolated phenomena; most of them seeming to exist in themselves and for themselves, rising and disappearing under changing conditions.... But opposed to the discontinuous Cosmos perceived, there is the invisible continuous Cosmos, which is conceived of as uniform Existence, all modes of which are interdependent, none permanent. The contradiction is palpable. On the one side there is ceaseless change and destruction, birth and death, on the other side destruction is only transformation, and the flux of change is the continuous manifestation of an indestructible, perdurable Existence. [II, pp. 28–29]

"The discontinuous Cosmos perceived" is the Victorian world without God, Newman's living busy world that shows "no trace of my creator." The wider the vision of relations, however, and the more broad the range of imagination, the more beautiful the world becomes. What Rosamond, with her narrow Middlemarchian mind, finds hideous and monstrous, her husband finds beautiful. "The invisible continuous Cosmos" offers not, of course, a "trace of my creator," but another object of verifiable empirical study—the organism. And organism, in late-century thought, almost displaces God, for its vital complexity can help explain phenomena that seem merely irrational and fortuitous. The organism offers an ultimately intelligible universe, and it banishes monsters. What appears as "destruction" becomes only "transformation," and what appears as the "flux of change" turns out to be "the continuous manifestation of an indestructible, perdurable Existence." Thus, within the same empiricist tradition by which Newman learned to make the leap from the limitation of sense experience to God, Lewes makes the leap from that limitation to science, and scientific method. Progress, the diminution of evil, follows directly from the expansion of science beyond simple empiricism to an exploration of the "unapparent" by means of the refined instruments of hypothesis, imagination, and sheer intellectual energy.

In *Middlemarch*, Lydgate is on the verge of the imaginative genius required for true application of scientific method, and he is most directly engaged in the attempt to see "unapparent relations." In that brilliant passage, so easily read as a description of the novelist's art," in which Lydgate's investigative ambitions are described, we learn that he values

the imagination that reveals subtle actions inaccessible by any sort of lens, but tracked in that outer darkness through long pathways of necessary sequence by the inward light which is the last refinement of Energy, capable of bathing even the etheral atoms in its ideally illuminated space. [p. 122]

Every word here is alive with scientific or Lewesian implication. This is no mere vague celebration of scientific hopes and tenacity, but a precise articulation of the dream of meaning, of the melding together of object and subject, self and other, thought (or spirit) and matter. It is where Lewesian empiricism, in its later phases, desired to go. It may be, as the narrator remarks, that Lydgate has asked the wrong questions in his investigations, but he is not far askew; and in this passage George Eliot implies Huxley's world governed according to rational laws and uniform principles. In it, all phenomena will be made comprehensible by a unifying theory.

—George Levine, *The Realistic Imagination: English Fiction from Frankenstein to Lady Chatterly*, (Chicago: The University of Chicago Press, 1981): 264–269.

Daniel Deronda

Set and structured as a biblical allegory, *Daniel Deronda* studies the emergence of moral lives in its two main characters, Gwendolyn Harleth and Daniel Deronda. Art figures prominently in this novel, attached directly and indirectly to religion and figured into several of the characters' lives—Miss Arrowpoint devotes herself to several instruments, Mirah is a singer, Daniel's estranged mother comes from a line of singers—and Gwendolen herself wishes to be an artist not least in order to broker the choice between poverty and marriage. The novel's double plot has been criticized for its lack of apparent unity. The two strains—the English strain, the story of Gwendolen Harleth, and the Jewish strain, the story of Daniel Deronda—are intertwined from the beginning, *in media res*, when the protagonists' eyes meet over a roulette table in Leubronn. Gwendolen Harleth is a beautiful, independent, wily young woman. When a letter alerting her of a failed business and her family's bankruptcy calls her back to England, she pawns a necklace to pay for the journey; when it is promptly and anonymously returned, she suspects that it's the work of the mysterious Deronda.

Before this point, Gwendolen's social circles have revolved around Offendene Manor, her temporary home and that of her Aunt and Uncle Gascoigne and her cousins Rex and Anna, and the Arrowpoints of Quetcham Hall, who are housing the well-regarded German musician, Klesmer, while he teaches their daughter Catherine. Rex falls in love with his cousin, and Gwendolen leads him to believe she may have feeling for him by conceding to go riding one day. When Rex's horse throws him and injures his leg, she laughs and rides off; she later rejects his proposal, contending she'll never marry. Heartbroken, Rex goes to Southampton for the rest of his vacation. The arrival of the wealthy and eligible bachelor Grandcourt, the nephew of Sir Hugo Mallinger of Diplow, stirs interest in the neighborhood and prompts speculation that he may wish to marry either Catherine Arrowpoint or Gwendolen. After he is introduced to all at an archery party, Grandcourt resolves to marry Gwendolen, who has little feeling for him, although she knows it would be a good match. Gwendolyn's decision is made, however, when a letter delivered to her by Grandcourt's steward, Lush, requests a meeting with a mysterious woman Lydia Glasher, who is the estranged mother of Grandcourt's four children and wishes her eldest to become Grandcourt's heir. Shocked, Gwendolyn vows not to interfere with Mrs. Glasher's wishes and flees for the Continent, resolved not to marry Grandcourt and disappointing her family, who thinks the marriage might have delivered them from poverty.

Meanwhile, Deronda's story unfolds—he is a striking man who calls Sir Hugo Mallinger "uncle" despite his unknown parentage. One evening in July, while rowing on the Thames, he encounters a despairing young Jewess named Mirah Lapidoth who has fled her demanding father in Prague and who is in search of her long-lost mother and brother named Ezra Cohen. Deronda brings Mirah to the mother of his friend Hans Meyrick; despite her disapproval of Jews, Mrs. Meyrick welcomes Mirah as one of her own. Mirah resolves to support herself by singing and to find her lost relatives.

Gwendolen decides that rather than marrying Grandcourt, she will work as a singer to earn money for her family. She is ultimately discouraged, however, by a visit to Klesmer, who has just become engaged to Catherine Arrowpoint against her family's will. Klesmer informs Gwendolyn that she lacks both the talent and purpose for such a calling. Resigned, Gwendolen concedes to marry Grandcourt, but she is wracked with guilt— she receives Grandcourt's diamonds from Mrs. Glasher, along with a note stating that Gwendolen's knowledge will be her curse.

Mirah becomes smitten by Deronda and continually mistakes him for a Jew. Walking in an unfashionable part of London, Deronda stumbles upon a shop with a sign that says "Ezra Cohen." There he finds a family he thinks too common to be relatives of Mirah. Still, he is fascinated by their Sabbath rituals and by a poor man named Mordecai—a guest of the Cohens.

Mr. and Mrs. Grandcourt visit Diplow and Gwendolen encounters Deronda again—they speak of the retrieved necklace, and their familiarity annoys the increasingly cold Grandcourt. Deronda accuses Gwendolen of being selfish, and she confesses she is ungrateful and implores him to tell her how to be better.

Hans Meyrick returns from Rome, and as Daniel fears, he falls in love with Mirah. Deronda speaks to Klesmer on Mirah's behalf and the musician agrees to teach her; she makes her debut at a party at Lady Mallinger's house. Deronda revisits Mordecai and, inspired by his intelligence and perception, begins reading the Talmud with him. Mordecai reveals that his name is Ezra, and shocked, Deronda realizes that this frail scholar is Mirah's brother—the news soon inspires a tearful reunion.

Grandcourt is growing increasingly suspicious of Gwendolen's relationship with Deronda. He concedes reluctantly to hire Mirah to sing at a party, but tells his wife he suspects Deronda of having false relations with the Jewess. Gwendolen goes to Mirah to hire her and asks if the rumors are true. Offended, Mirah accepts the invitation but cuts short the conversation. Grandcourt rebukes Gwendolen for the visit and informs her that Lush is to go over Grandcourt's will with her. Gwendolen learns that in the event she doesn't have a son, Mrs. Glasher's eldest, Henleigh, will be heir. Despite the tension in their relationship, Grandcourt insists on taking her yachting—they travel until the skipper informs them they'll have to stay a week in Genoa.

Meanwhile, Sir Hugo has given a shocked Deronda a letter from his ill mother, the Princess Halm-Eberstein. She asks him to visit her in Genoa. When they meet, she reveals he is a Jew—that she was forced to marry his father, her cousin; that she chose a life of independence and separation from her faith that would allow her to pursue her career as a singer. She insists that she did not want her son to grow up with the burdens and prejudices of Judaism. She tells him that his grandfather's chest is in Mainz, where a friend, Joseph Kalonymos, will meet him. Deronda later reveals that he is in love with a Jewess and his mother, disapproving, tells him she lacks the capability to love. They part with the acknowledgment that they'll never see one another again. Deronda encounters Gwendolen on the staircase of the hotel, raises his hat, and passes on—she is begrudgingly on her way to a sailing expedition. Not long after, Deronda sees a boat being rowed ashore by two men and Gwendolen inside, pale and shivering. Shaken, she tells Deronda Grandcourt is dead. Later, she confesses that she'd had it in her mind to kill him for awhile, and when he fell off the boat, she didn't move to save him. The provisions of Grandcourt's will are soon revealed—Mrs. Glasher's son will be heir to the fortune and Gwendolyn will be given two-thousand a year and a modest house in the coal-fields, where Mrs. Glasher had been living.

Deronda confesses to Sir Hugo that the revelation of his true origin will have a profound impact on his life. Deronda goes to Mainz, visits Kalonymos, and learns that his grandfather, Daniel Charisi, comes from a line of Spanish Jews who preserved manuscripts of the family lineage. On her way home one day Mirah encounters her father, Mr. Lapidoth—he asks for money and support and though she wants nothing to do with him, she invites him in. He tells her he will return the next day and asks for money. Mordecai insists that they have been betrayed and that their father will not be allowed to return. Deronda comes and tells them of his revelations—his news is received with much joy, and Mordecai insists Deronda call him Ezra. Meanwhile, however, Mirah has become suspicious that Deronda is in love with Gwendolen.

Gwendolen sends for Deronda and asks him what she should do, saying she wants to be good. Deronda advises her to be kind to others and to love purpose. A discussion with her uncle and with Sir Hugo results in Gwendolen's settling in Offendene—the prospect of settling in the house she once despised fills her with relief. Meanwhile, Mr. Lapidoth returns to Mirah at home. Ezra sends his sister out of the room and strongly rebukes his father, but tells him that he may stay. Deronda approaches a haggard-looking Hans for advice. Hans admits to smoking opium and Deronda reveals his heritage and says he plans to travel East. They discuss Deronda's love for Mirah, and Hans encourages him. Deronda visits Ezra and Mirah again and realizes that his ring is missing. As Mirah and Deronda go to find Mr. Lapidoth, whom they fear has stolen the ring, Deronda proposes to her. During a later visit, Daniel reveals to Gwendolen his parentage and his plans to marry Mirah and move East. Gwendolen replies she has been forsaken, that she has been a cruel woman; but she says she has been better for knowing Deronda. She later tells her mother that she will live. Ezra passes away quietly, before the three can embark on their trip, with Mirah and Deronda's arms around him.

Daniel Deronda

The female protagonist of the novel, **Gwendolen Harleth** is used to getting what she wants. Intelligent and beautiful, she is also selfish—though she is not in love with Grandcourt, she finally accepts his proposal because doing so will provide her family with financial stability. She is in love with Deronda and to the chagrin of her husband continually seeks him out, soliciting his advice.

Gwendolen's doting mother is **Fanny Davilow**. She believes she made a poor second marriage, and after her husband's death, she is forced to rely on her sister and brother in law, Mr. and Mrs. Gascoigne.

Mrs. Gascoigne is Mrs. Davilow's sister and Gwendolyn's aunt. Darker and slighter than her sister, she believes she has been the luckier one. Together, she and her husband make sacrifices to support her sister's family during their time of need.

The kind and authoritative Rector of Pennicote, **Mr. Gascoigne** believes Gwendolen will make a brilliant marriage and therefore takes pains to introduce her to local society.

Small, timid **Anna Gascoigne** is supposed to be a playmate for Gwendolyn, but her elder cousin ends up upstaging her. She has a powerful devotion to her brother, Rex and a distaste for the manners and methods of society women.

Rex Gascoigne is Anna's intelligent, hardworking brother. He falls in love with Gwendolen but is eventually rejected by her.

Mrs. Arrowpoint, despite her squat-figure and parrot-like voice, is believed to have been a woman of fortune. She believes herself to have literary tendencies, and keeps busy writing books.

Catherine Arrowpoint plays three instruments but does not sing, as Gwendolen does. Her teacher, Herr Klesmer, falls in love with her, and the two marry against her parents' will.

Herr Klesmer is a German Jew and a gifted professor of music. He is hired by the Arrowpoints to teach Catherine and eventually marries her. Klesmer discourages Gwendolen from pursuing a career in music, saying that she is not devoted enough, but encourages Mirah.

Grandcourt is the nephew of Sir Hugo Mallinger and presumptive heir to his baronetcy. Cold and unfeeling, he uses the people in his life, from his steward, Mr. Lush, to his wife.

Mr. Lush is the traveling companion of Grandcourt who is often ill-treated by his boss. His allegiance to Mrs. Lydia Glasher, Grandcourt's former mistress, prompts him to arrange a meeting between her and Gwendolen to discourage Gwendolen's marrying Grandcourt.

Mrs. Lydia Glasher is the scorned mother of Grandcourt's four children. She is kept at a modest house and wishes that her eldest son Heinleigh be made heir of Grandcourt's fortune.

Daniel Deronda is a man of uncertain parentage and the ward of Sir Hugo Mallinger. He encounters Gwendolen Harleth in Leubronn and saves Mirah from drowning herself in the Thames.

Mirah Lapidoth is a young Jewess first encountered by Deronda when distraught over her father's mistreatment and despairing over her estranged mother and brother, she tries to drown herself in the Thames. A talented vocalist, she studies with Klesmer and sings at neighborhood gatherings.

Ezra Cohen is a Jewish shopkeeper whom Deronda believes to be Mirah's long-lost brother. In his tiny flat, Deronda encounters his entire family and witnesses his first bit of Jewish ritual.

Mordecai is a poor, frail, but learned Jew whose real name is Ezra Mordecai Cohen. Before it is revealed that he is Mirah's brother, Ezra Cohen's family cares him for him.

Mrs. Meryick, the mother of Hans and a good-natured Christian woman of modest means, nurtures Mirah among her children.

Hans Meyrick is a friend of Deronda's and a painter. He falls in love with Mirah, despite the fact that she's a Jewess.

Princess Halm-Eberstein is Deronda's biological mother, who reveals herself near the end of her life. She wanted to devote herself to her singing and therefore freed herself of her Judaism, her family, and her son.

Joseph Kalonymos is a friend of Deronda's grandfather, Daniel Charisi, whom Deronda visits in Mainz in order to obtain his inheritance.

Mr. Lapidoth is Mirah's father. He brought his daughter around the world while he tried his fortune as an actor, and even when it wasn't beneficial to Mirah, he encouraged her to make sacrifices for a life in the theater. He is a selfish opportunist who later tries to exploits the kindness of his daughter and estranged son.

CRITICAL VIEWS ON
Daniel Deronda

BARBARA HARDY ON UNITY IN REPEATED IMAGERY

[Barbara Hardy is the author of *Particularities: Readings in George Eliot*, *The Novels of George Eliot*, and *The Exposure of Luxury: Radical Themes in Thackeray*. Here, she discusses the effectiveness of Eliot's use of repeated imagery in the novel, specifically of horses and widening horizons.]

[T]here is another recurring image in *Daniel Deronda* which is of the ironical stuff of the central images of *Middlemarch*. It is also an animal image, though this time it is taken from an animal which has a real existence within the novel. This is the image of the horse or the chariot drawn by horses. Katherine Mansfield noticed the passionate effect of Stephen's panting horse in *The Mill on the Floss*, and the images in *Daniel Deronda* were also anticipated by one image in *Felix Holt*, where Esther, a Gwendolen who escapes her Grandcourt, has her possible fate described by Mrs Transome, who speaks with authority:

> This girl has a fine spirit—plenty of fire and pride and wit. Men like such captives, as they like horses that champ the bit and paw the ground: they feel more triumph in their mastery. (Ch. xxxix.)

This image is repeated, with ironical flexibility, throughout *Daniel Deronda*. Its source within the novel is obvious and appropriate, for Gwendolen's imperious egoism, her ruthlessness, and her love of splendour are all shown, carefully and separately, in some episode concerned with riding on horses. The princess in exile, she demands a fine horse. She rides to hounds and leaves Rex to ride after her, for a fall. Her courtship by Grandcourt is almost entirely equestrian. When she has accepted him they go to the window to see the horse Criterion:

They could see the two horses being taken slowly round the sweep, and the beautiful creatures, in their fine grooming, sent a thrill of exultation through Gwendolen. They were the symbols of command and luxury, in delightful contrast with the ugliness of poverty and humiliation at which she had lately been looking close. (Ch. xxvii.)

This is the suggestive object in literal existence, but the horse has another life in metaphor. What Gwendolen does in fact she plays with in imagination, and the modulation from the real horses to the horses in imagery seems hardly noticeable. When she is first considering marriage with Grandcourt:

Gwendolen wished to mount the chariot and drive the plunging horses herself, with a spouse by her side who would fold his arms and give her his countenance without looking ridiculous. (Ch. xiii.)

The image recurs just before she accepts Grandcourt, when she moves in mind from one alternative to another:

Meanwhile, the thought that he was coming to be refused was inspiriting: she had the white reins in her hands again. (Ch. xxvii.)

But when we next meet the image of the horse it is with a difference, for it is now the image in Grandcourt's fantasy:

She had been brought to accept him in spite of everything—brought to kneel down like a horse under training for the arena, though she might have an objection to it all the while. (Ch. xxviii.)

The clash of the separated images has its own tension, and gives life to Grandcourt's desire, which is not a crude desire for mastery, but a more sophisticated desire to master the woman who would have liked to master him, and who perhaps would have been capable of mastering another man. The coincidence of the images makes the oblique statement that two can play at metaphors. Gwendolen's image of mastering horses turns into Grandcourt's vision of her as a mastered horse.

The clash of images continues; Gwendolen is forced to change hers:

> It was as if she had consented to mount a chariot where another held the reins; and it was not in her nature to leap out in the eyes of the world. (Ch. xxix.)

And, six pages later in the same chapter:

> The horses in the chariot she had mounted were going at full speed.

This is before her marriage. Afterwards, the images fall off, existing, like the contrast between fountain and pond, to make an ironical contrast which ends with the heroine's awakening. Grandcourt comes to observe that she answered to the rein (ch. XXXV): not only is she not holding the reins, but she is being driven, and towards the end he feels "perfectly satisfied that he held his wife with bit and bridle" (ch. LIV). This silent struggle in imagery is joined only once by another character—Deronda seems to hear Gwendolen's trust call out "as if it had been the retreating cry of a creature snatched and carried out of his reach by swift horsemen" (ch. L).

Deronda and Gwendolen share another image. This is again an experience with literal existence, the experience of wide space, which has the dual life of fact and metaphor. We meet it first in a metaphor so familiar that it is unremarkable. Klesmer is attacking Gwendolen's music:

> "It is a form of melody which expresses a puerile state of culture—a dandling, canting, see-saw kind of stuff—the passion and thought of people without any breadth of horizon. There is a sort of self-satisfied folly about every phrase of such melody: no cries of deep, mysterious passion—no conflict—no sense of the universal. It makes men small as they listen to it. Sing now something larger. And I shall see."
>
> "Oh, not now—by-and-by," said Gwendolen, with a sinking of heart at the sudden width of horizon.... (Ch. v.)

Klesmer's rebuke is the first slight felt by Gwendolen's self-satisfaction, but her fear of the widening horizon is shown as a peculiarity of her sensibility, as well as a natural consequence of being the spoilt princess:

> Solitude in any wide scene impressed her with an undefined feeling of immeasurable existence aloof from her, in the midst of which she was helplessly incapable of asserting herself. The little astronomy taught her at school used sometimes to set her imagination at work in a way that made her tremble: but always when some one joined her she recovered her indifference to the vastness in which she seemed an exile. (Ch. vi.)

The relation between Deronda and Gwendolen depends very much, I believe, on our acceptance of the prominence of this theme, which establishes in imagery and in actual landscape the difference between the two, the need Gwendolen has for dependence, and the measure of her final solitude. Deronda, like Klesmer, attacks her narrowness, tries to make her understand the possibility of non-attachment, and behind the flatness of precept is his experience.

> He chose a spot in the bend of the river just opposite Kew Gardens, where he had a great breadth of water before him reflecting the glory of the sky, while he himself was in shadow. He lay with his hands behind his head propped on a level with the boat's edge, so that he could see all around him, but could not be seen by any one at a few yards' distance; and for a long while he never turned his eyes from the view right in front of him. He was forgetting everything else in a half-speculative, half-involuntary identification of himself with the objects he was looking at, thinking how far it might be possible habitually to shift his centre till his own personality would be no less outside him than the landscape. (Ch. xvii.)

There is a link here with Mordecai, whose "imagination spontaneously planted him on some spot where he had a far-reaching scene; his thought went on in wide spaces" (ch. XXXVIII). This delight in wide spaces is made suggestive of the breadth of vision, the altruist's out-turned look. It is, on a larger scale, the outward gaze through the window which stamps the renunciations of Esther Lyon and Dorothea. What is triumph for them is also triumph for Gwendolen, though for her it is the cathartic shock. Just as her vision of the insect face and the dead face in the picture came to have an actual presence, like Mordecai's vision of the bridge, so her terror in wide spaces becomes an actual nightmare. This is the last image which, in its echo of what we have heard before, completes the fantasy and fixes the moral:

> There was a long silence between them. The world seemed getting larger round poor Gwendolen, and she more solitary and helpless in the midst. The thought that he might come back after going to the East, sank before the bewildering vision of these wide-stretching purposes in which she felt herself reduced to a mere speck ... she was for the first time feeling the pressure of a vast mysterious movement, for the first time being dislodged from her supremacy in her own world, and getting a sense that her horizon was but a dipping onward of an existence with which her own was revolving. (Ch. lxix.)

I began by emphasizing the unity built by these repeated images. Perhaps I should end by emphasizing their effect of inevitability, seen nowhere so clearly as in *Daniel Deronda*. George Eliot is clearly working away from a full use of omniscient commentary, skilfully managed though this is in her novels, towards the indirect methods of hinting images. Once we find the trail the purpose is clear though the hints are often embedded in passages which we probably read more carelessly than we read the conversations or spotlighted action.

—Barbara Hardy, "Imagery in George Eliot's Last Novels," *Discussions of George Eliot*, ed. Richard Stang, (Boston: D.C. Heath and Company, 1960): 82–84.

MARTIN PRICE ON THE OPENING SCENE

[Martin Price is Professor of English at Yale University. He is the author of *Swift's Rhetorical Art* and *To the Palace of Wisdom* and the co-editor of the *Oxford Anthology of American Literature*. Here he discusses the themes of the novel in relation to the opening scene.]

In her last novel, George Eliot studied the emergence of a moral life in Gwendolen Harleth and the descent upon Daniel Deronda of an idea which can give the energy of duty to undirected moral aspiration. Eliot opens the novel with the first meeting of these two. The opening chapters of *Daniel Deronda* are intense and mysterious, mysterious because we have no knowledge of the conditions from which these events arise. "Was she beautiful or not beautiful? and what was the secret of form or expression which gave the dynamic quality of her glance? Was the good or evil genius dominant in those beams?" We see Gwendolen Harleth as Daniel Deronda first sees her; she is gambling in the casino of a German watering place, and her manner conveys "unrest," strange agitation. Her double aspect—both the physical beauty and the tortured spirit—compel Deronda's attention, but compel it against his will. "Why was his wish to look again felt as coercion and not as a longing with which the whole being consents?" Much later—some eight hundred pages later—we shall look back at the "mission of Deronda to Gwendolen" which "had begun with what she had felt to be his judgment of her at the gaming-table" (64).

This opening scene is presented externally, with the swaggering mockery of Dickens. The casino is a resort "which the enlightenment of ages has prepared ... at a heavy cost of gilt mouldings, dark-toned colour and chubby nudities, all correspondingly heavy—forming a suitable condenser for human breath belonging, in great part, to the highest fashion.... It was near four o'clock on a September day, so that the atmosphere was well brewed to a visible haze." This haze has the disturbing concreteness, and the gamblers are picked out with the contemptuous precision, that Dickens often uses:

> the white bejewelled fingers of an English countess were very near touching a bony, yellow, crab-like hand stretching a bared wrist to clutch a heap of coin—a hand easy to sort with the square, gaunt face, deep-set eyes, grizzled eyebrows, and ill-combed scanty hair which seemed a slight metamorphosis of the vulture.

Among the attitudes the gamblers reveal are the rankling "sweetness of winning much and seeing others lose" and the "fierce yet tottering impulsiveness" of the man who plays by an insane system, like a "scene of dull, gas-poisoned absorption." Later Deronda will reveal his view of gambling: "There is something revolting to me in raking a heap of money together, and internally chuckling over it, when others are feeling the loss" (29).

Gwendolen plays willfully, restlessly, exulting as she wins, but suddenly arrested to find herself under Deronda's gaze. She has a momentary sense that he is "measuring her and looking down on her as an inferior, ... examining her as a species of a lower order." Her resentment prolongs her stare in turn, until she looks away as if with "inward defiance." Gwendolen has begun to imagine herself a "goddess of luck." But that fantasy is crossed by her uneasy awareness of Deronda's gaze—it seems to express a scorn that, at a deeper level, she suspects she deserves, and therefore resents all the more. Under its influence, her luck changes. She defies Deronda, still feeling his eyes upon her although she cannot turn to face him. If she cannot win, she will at least lose "strikingly" (1).

This evening marks an epoch for Gwendolen (and to a degree for Deronda). She has fled England rather than undertake a marriage she has seen to be degrading. Now she discovers, upon her return to her hotel, that her family has lost all its money. When she pawns a necklace with the thought that she may recover her magical luck, she is outraged and shamed that Deronda observes what she has done, redeems the necklace, and sends it back to her. She has begun to find in him a judgment of herself which she guiltily supposes to be superior and ironic. His judgment will in time become, once she recognizes its genuine concern and affection, her conscience. At last she will have internalized that judgment and made it her protection against herself. As she says to Deronda, "it shall be better with me because I have known you" (36, 70).

—Martin Price, *Forms of Life: Character and Moral Imagination in the Novel*, (New Haven: Yale University Press, 1983): 164–165.

MARY WILSON CARPENTER ON DIVISION OF CHRISTIAN
AND JEWISH PROPHECY

[Mary Wilson Carpenter is the author of *George Eliot and
the Landscape of Time: Narrative Form and Protestant
Apocalyptic History* and has written essays on Frances
Trollope and Christina Rossetti. Here she discusses how
it relates to the double plot construction of the novel
relates to the Victorian version of Christian dualistic
history and the Book of Daniel.]

The double aspect of *Daniel Deronda* obviously resembles this
prophetic structure of history. Gwendolen's narrative represents
the English or Christian stream of history, Daniel's the Jewish.
Opening in medias res, at the gambling resort in Leubronn, the
narrative immediately focuses on Daniel's judgment of
Gwendolen: "Was she beautiful or not beautiful? ... Was the
good or the evil genius dominant?" Daniel's function here, as
elsewhere in the novel, is to interpret the moral or spiritual value
of Gwendolen's history. Like the Hebrew prophets, he
pronounces judgment on this Gentile and later exhorts her to
repentance and regeneration. Daniel's advice and counsel to
Gwendolen repeatedly bridge the two narratives, which conclude
with Gwendolen's humble acknowledgment of Daniel's
transforming influence on her: "it shall be better with me
because I have known you" (882).

The double-narrative structure of the novel, then, bears an
interestingly close resemblance to this Victorian version of
Christian dualistic history, traditionally associated with the Book
of Daniel. The novel differs in one important respect, however:
it reverses the moral position of Jew and Christian. George Eliot
has ironized her historical model, for in the novel it is the
English Christian stream that must be "converted" and restored
to the great river of human history by Hebrew prophetic vision.
The narrative solidly identifies the downward progress of
worldly empire with the English "half," whereas the Jewish
"half," dominated by Daniel, Mordecai, and Mirah, represents
visionary growth and progress. Although the Meyricks, for

example, provide a refuge for Mirah, she converts *them* to a wider sympathy, exposing the narrowness of their Evangelical beliefs. And Mrs. Mallinger, who supports the Society for the Conversion of the Jews and devoutly hopes Mirah will embrace Christianity, lives instead to see her husband's adopted son embrace Judaism as well as this Jewish maiden (267).

Instructive and even amusing though it may be to compare *Daniel Deronda* with this Victorian version of dualistic history, the comparison does not in itself suggest how we could read the novel, in the words George Eliot quoted, as "one great whole." If *Daniel Deronda* functions in part as an ironic allegory of traditional Christian history, then its two plot lines come together only in the last chapter, and then only in prophetic types of an eventual "restoration" of the Jews and "conversion" of the Gentiles. The narratives, like Davison's structure of prophetic history, would not coalesce until some "apocalypse" beyond their time frame. This aspect of Danielic commentary, though it suggests a model and a rationale for George Eliot's separation of the narrative into two plot lines, fails to explain how the reader might be expected to relate everything in the novel to everything else—at least within its temporal realm.

Further investigation of the Victorian literature on Daniel, however, suggests a more complex conception of dualistic history that not only unites the two streams within a "universal history" but also points to the presence of an "apocalypse" in the text—a symbolic conversion that identifies Christian with Jew and bonds future with past. George Eliot produces that universal history in the text of *Daniel Deronda* through her appropriation of the Prophecy of the Seventy Weeks. The Old Testament prophecy serves as the dominant structuring metaphor in this novel, in contrast to its more limited narrative functions in *Romola* and *Middlemarch*. But to interpret this structure, the reader must first be familiar with the general features of "continuous historical" and typological interpretation of the seventy weeks—the interpretation traditional in the Victorian Anglican church. (...)

Obviously, both Deronda's name and "love of universal history" suggest the Book of Daniel, traditionally, seen as the major prophecy of the Babylonian exile (220). Like Daniel the prophet, Deronda lives in "exile"—an exile from knowledge of his origin—and like the prophet, he becomes adviser to a Gentile, interpreter of a "dream" or vision that causes great spiritual turmoil. Modern readers are less likely to realize that Mordecai is also an exilic name, for in the Book of Esther a Jew named Mordecai advises his niece to marry the Persian ruler and thus enables her later to save her people from destruction. The Book of Esther may in fact have contributed more than the name of a character to the novel, for in the tale gambling, or the casting of lots, represents at first the seemingly haphazard fate of those disinherited or "exiled" but later the prophetic destiny attained through active choice of one's heritage—an obvious parallel to the emblematic theme of gambling in the novel.

Mordecai's other name, Ezra, has even stronger links to the literature of exile, for Ezra led the Jews in their return from the Babylonian exile. Names from earlier exiles also appear in the novel. Both Mordecai and Klesmer are compared to Elijah, the prophet whose forty-day exile in the desert exegetes read as a type of Christ's forty days of temptation in the wilderness. Both Mirah and Lydia Glasher are similarly compared to Hagar, Abraham's disinherited wife, who was driven into the desert with her son, Ishmael. Even the angelic machinery of this novel suggests a subtle link to the literature of exile, for not only is the angel Gabriel—mentioned twice in the novel—the angel in the Book of Daniel, but Daniel is the first biblical work to name angels.

George Eliot's "landscape of exile" thus draws on names, characters, and even themes from the biblical literature of exile. That landscape, as Sudrann has demonstrated, characterizes both plot lines, for Daniel and Gwendolen are each exiled from their origins: lack of a "homeland," of a known birthplace, deprives them of a spiritual inheritance that would give shape and moral significance to their own lives. But George Eliot primarily exploits the numerological symbolism of exile to write Daniel and Gwendolen's individual histories as a united, prophetic history of humanity in exile. As in *Romola* (and to a lesser extent in *Middlemarch* and *Adam Bede*), the numbering of chapters becomes an integral part of the hermeneutic design of the narrative. But whereas in the earlier novels the numerological implications of chapter numbers chiefly reflect exegesis of the Book of Revelation, in *Daniel Deronda* they seem to allude specifically to interpretations of the Book of Daniel. To begin with, the seventy chapters of the novel suggest a structural analogue to the Prophecy of the Seventy Weeks.

> —Mary Wilson Carpenter, *George Eliot and the Landscape of Time: Narrative Form and Protestant Apocalyptic History*, (Chapel Hill: The University of North Carolina Press, 1986): 135–136; 138–139.

DOROTHEA BARRETT ON CAPITALISM AND THE IMAGE OF THE CHOIR STABLES

[Dorothea Barrett has edited the Penguin edition of *Romola* and is the author of *Vocation and Desire: George Eliot's Heroines*. Here, she discusses dwindling social values within the images of the casino and the choir stables.]

George Eliot sees human and cultural values as dwindling in inverse proportion to the growth of capitalism and imperialism. Having realized, in the creation of Gwendolen, that people are not like Dinah, Romola, and Dorothea, spiritual in the extreme and to the point of implausibility, she further realizes that the growing consumerism of British culture is making it less and less possible for people to be spiritual to any degree whatsoever. This is expressed in a remarkable series of images that shows the human and spiritual being converted into commodities and is chillingly prophetic of the Nazi prison camp manufactories of the Second World War.

> 'And, my dear boy, it is good to be unselfish and generous; but don't carry that too far. It will not do to give yourself to be melted down for the benefit of the tallow-trade.'
> (I: 275)

> Knowledge, through patient and frugal centuries, enlarges discovery and makes a record of it; Ignorance, wanting its day's dinner, lights a fire with the record, and gives a flavour to its one roast with the burnt souls of many centuries.
> (I: 340)

'No man,' says a Rabbi, by way of indisputable instance, 'may turn the bones of his father and mother into spoons.'
(II: 156)

'the Gentile, who had said, "What is yours is ours, and no longer yours," was reading the letter of our law as a dark inscription, or was turning its parchments into shoe-laces for an army rabid with lust and cruelty.'
(II: 386)

The gambling casino and the choir-stables are variations on the same idea: the cannibalistic nature of the spreading capitalist ideology, and the way in which cultural, human, and spiritual values are supplanted by commodity value. On the metaphorical level, the description of the casino can also be seen as prophetic. In it, the eroding of class and cultural barriers by the commonality of money-lust under advanced capitalism is predicted with irony:

There too, very near the fair countess, was a respectable London tradesman ... conscious of circulars addressed to the nobility and gentry, whose distinguished patronage enabled him to take his holidays fashionably, and to a certain extent in their distinguished company. Not his the gambler's passion that nullifies appetite, but a well-fed leisure, which in the intervals of winning money in business and spending it show-ily, sees no better resource than winning money in play and spending it yet more showily—reflecting always that Providence had never manifested any disapprobation of his amusement, and dispassionate enough to leave off if the sweet-ness of winning much and seeing others lose had turned to the sourness of losing much and seeing others win. For the vice of gambling lay in losing money at it.
(I: 6)

Gambling, like bourgeois individualism, both highlights individuality and breaks down the divisive barriers of cultures and classes by giving members of different cultures and classes the common and uniting interest of competing for money:

But while every single player differed markedly from every other, there was a certain uniform negativeness of expression which had the effect of a mask—as if they had all eaten of some root that for the time compelled the brains of each to the same narrow monotony of action.

(I: 6–7)

The paradox implicit in this uniting to compete is both ironic and profoundly discouraging: money-lust manages to achieve what belief-systems, from Christianity to communism, have attempted with little success:

Here certainly was a striking admission of human equality. The white bejewelled fingers of an English countess were very near touching a bony, yellow, crab-like hand stretching a bared wrist to clutch a heap of coin.

(I: 6)

The image of choir-stables (chapter 35) expresses the same idea in different form and links that idea into the dominant metaphoric network of the novel. Throughout the George Eliot canon, as elsewhere in literature, attitudes to horse-riding are used as a metaphor for sexuality. Here, as Barbara Hardy has pointed out, both Gwendolen and Grandcourt see marriage as horse-riding (Hardy 1959: 228)—the self in the role of rider and the other in the role of horse. Gwendolen moves from a pleasant anticipation of mounting to the uncomfortable realization of being mounted. This is a double-edged metaphor: on the level of power struggle, Gwendolen is unpleasantly surprised to find herself dominated where she had hoped to dominate; on the level of sexual symbolism, the sexual aversion we witnessed in her repulse of Rex (I: 117–19) becomes sexual terror as she realizes that Grandcourt's coldness does not, as she had thought, exempt her from sexual obligations in marriage but rather obliges her to be subjected to cold, power-seeking, and loveless sex. Meanwhile the jewel imagery which has developed side by side with the horse-riding imagery fuses with it brilliantly, as Lloyd Fernando has pointed out, when Gwendolen realizes that the diamond necklace, which represents Grandcourt's wealth and aristocracy and is associated with his illegitimate family by Mrs Glasher (itself a privilege of his wealth and aristocracy), has become the reins with which Grandcourt controls and dominates Gwendolen herself (Fernando 1977: 59).

In this metaphoric context, the choir-stables suggest not only the decline of the church as it is displaced by a growing consumerism (Garrett 1969: 1–4) but also a parallel and related decline of the sacredness of marriage as it is displaced by a growing objectification of the marriage partner. Grandcourt sees Gwendolen as a commodity to be acquired and used for her sexual and ornamental value; Gwendolen sees Grandcourt as a commodity to be acquired and used for his monetary and prestige value. Deronda, by contrast, takes his hat off to the horses, suggesting reserves of reverence in him that have been eroded in everyone else: reverence for religion; reverence for human love; reverence for all the spiritual and human values that are being slowly usurped by the growing consumerism of English culture.

This is the dehumanizing cultural milieu in which Gwendolen is located. It bears no resemblance to earlier George Eliot worlds. Hayslope, St Ogg's, Raveloe, and Middlemarch may have had their faults, their narrow prejudices, harsh judgements, suffocating limitations, but they were nevertheless human communities for which it was possible to feel affection and even a grudging respect. The web imagery describing these communities suggests both suffocating restriction (as in spiders' webs) and a sense of security, belonging, and relationship (Beer 1983: 149–80). The broad international setting of *Daniel Deronda* and the consumerism which characterizes it preclude any feeling of community, much less of the kind of community that can be described as an organic mesh. This new world, a world that anticipates the alienated settings of modernism, poses new problems for George Eliot in both the characterization and the destiny of its heroine. Once this medium has been defined, it becomes obvious that no Dinah, Romola, or Dorothea could possibly inhabit it. It also becomes apparent that George Eliot's old solutions to the life problems of her heroines, the role of ministering angel in which we last see Janet, in 'Janet's repentance', and Romola, and the role of wife and mother in which we last see Dinah and Dorothea, depend upon the existence of an organic human community and a strong sense of family. Both these are absent from the English world of *Daniel Deronda*. In this novel, families are fragmented or malformed (Welsh 1984: 319). Of all the families in the novel, only the Meyricks and the Cohens give the impression of intimate and nourishing family life, but they are separated, both by the class structure of English society and by the structure of the novel, from Gwendolen's world: they inhabit a middle social stratum, which is still relatively untouched by the alienation that has infected the gentry and aristocracy, and they inhabit the Jewish half of the novel, in which George Eliot still allows herself to paint and believe in possibility of the ideal.

> —Dorothea Barrett, *Vocation and Desire: George Eliot's Heroines*, (London: Routledge, 1989): 160–164.

DEIRDRE DAVID ON GWENDOLEN'S ATTACHMENT TO HER MOTHER

[Deirdre David is Professor of English at Temple University and author of *Fictions of Resolution in Three Victorian Novels*, *Intellectual Women and Victorian Patriarchy*, and *Rule Britannia: Women, Empire, and Victorian Writing*. Here she discusses Gwendolen's sexuality in relation to Freud.]

The problem for Gwendolen is that she has not detached herself from her mother. I do not mean this as a glib reduction of the complexity of fictive characterisation to neurotic symptom, but rather that Eliot's descriptions of Gwendolen's relationship with her mother are so intuitively suggestive of what Freud formulates into theory, so rich in that psychological analysis which Leslie Stephen suggests we might want to skip, that one can make a psychoanalytic reading of Gwendolen Harleth without implying that this is all there is to be said about her.

Gwendolen is tormented by the terrible actualisation of her fantasies of wishing her own father and her stepfather out of the picture in order that she may retain her mother for herself. In marrying Grandcourt she displaces a wronged woman, Lydia Glasher, who in many ways resembles her mother, and at the same time she thereby situates herself in the position of a punished female; she *becomes* her mother in an unconscious attempt to be punished and to be consequently discharged of her guilt. And in a massively cathected act, *she* becomes the child's first love-object and Grandcourt becomes *her*; he takes over the role of primitive male, which is the role she has played for so long in a household of women.

In describing Gwendolen's domestic tyranny, Eliot says that she is one of those people who possess "a strong determination to have what was pleasant, with a total fearlessness in making themselves disagreeable or dangerous when they did not get it. Who is so much cajoled and served with trembling by the weak females of a household as the unscrupulous male—capable, if he has not free way at home of going and doing worse elsewhere?" (Ch. 4). Now Gwendolen cannot go elsewhere and do worse, and she is obviously not an unscrupulous male, but much of the time she certainly behaves like one, which is what Eliot is implying here. She is the daughter of her mother's first marriage, and she lords it over her mother and four half-sisters, the daughters of one Captain Davilow who joined his family during his lifetime, "in brief and fitful manner, enough to reconcile them to his long absences" (Ch. 3). Gwendolen's function in the Offendene household is quickly apprehended by the new housekeeper when she remarks to the lady's maid that Gwendolen is the one "that's to command us all".

As a child of twelve she asks her mother, "Why did you marry again, mamma? It would have been nicer if you had not," and as an adult she sleeps on a couch next to her mother's bed, described by Eliot as a "catafalque". In her notes to *Daniel Deronda*, Barbara Hardy suggests that this is a heavy-handed joke on Eliot's part about the Victorian best bed, but I think it is also an oblique reference to the bed as a memorial of the sexual demands which have been made upon Mrs Davilow and which seem to have done her in. She is a worn and wasted woman, exhausted by the burden of four incipiently marriageable daughters, and alternately delighted and intimidated by the caprices of a fifth who behaves more like an "unscrupulous male" than a properly subdued young lady. Gwendolen has taken on the function of a third husband in her mother's household, one of the gratifications of such a role being that she thereby reconstructs, however unconsciously, that stage of pre-Oedipal sexual development when the father is out of the picture.

In "Female Sexuality", Freud describes one effect of the castration complex upon a girl:

> ... she clings in obstinate self-assertion to her threatened mas-
> culinity; the hope of getting a penis sometime is cherished to
> an incredibly late age and becomes the aim of her life, whilst
> the phantasy of really being a man in spite of everything, often
> dominates long periods of her life.

Gwendolen, if not exactly indulging in fantasies that she is a man, exhibits characteristics which are conventionally associated with male behaviour. She is aggressive in public (at least until she matches up with Grandcourt), and she is forceful in her private dealings with her family. Her fantasies are schoolboy ones of killing tigers and exploring the North-West Passage and her imperialistic way of handling the world is a cultural mark of male behaviour. I want to make a distinction here, by the way, between what might be interpreted as a feminist consciousness and a compulsion to situate oneself in the position of controlling one's mother. Gwendolen is no feminist self-projection for George Eliot; she wants, vicariously, to play the roles of husband and father.

Freud concludes his exposition of the difficulties experienced by girls in detaching themselves from their mothers and taking their fathers as a love-object by suggesting that a girl may follow "a very circuitous path whereby she arrives at the ultimate normal feminine attitude in which she takes her father as love-object, and thus arrives at the Oedipus complex in its feminine form".

This is no place to introduce arguments about what constitutes "the ultimate normal feminine attitude", or to quarrel with Freud's teleological notion of the road to sexual normality. I am more concerned with a correspondence between Eliot's fictive female and Freud's hypotheses because that correspondence seems to illuminate some of the relation between cultural arrest in *Daniel Deronda* and the psycho-sexual arrest of its heroine. At the end of *Daniel Deronda*, Gwendolen puts her foot on Freud's path to the Oedipus complex: she has taken Deronda as an ideal love-object and invested him with all the moral authority and protective capabilities of the father. And Gwendolen's diminished egoism, her calm admission to Deronda that because of having known him she "may live to be one of the best of women, who makes others glad that they were born", suggests that she has also put her foot on the path to an improved moral life. Gwendolen and the culture for which she is a metaphor may, therefore, both be said to move, however slightly and ambiguously, from a point of stasis.

Gwendolen's dread of adult sexuality is demonstrated in her response to Rex Gascoigne's gentlemanly advances. His presence makes her want to curl up like a sea-anemone; she shudders and cries, "Pray don't make love to me! I hate it." Her mother comes in to find Gwendolen sobbing bitterly and Eliot's description of Mrs Davilow's feelings suggests something of the unusual nature of the relationship between mother and daughter. She feels "something of the alarmed anguish that women feel at the sight of over-powering sorrow in a strong man; for this child had been her ruler". Gwendolen clings to her mother, crying, "I can't bear any one to be very near me but you," (Ch. 7) but in marrying Grandcourt she is obliged to have someone more than very near to her. He is an experienced sexual aggressor, and she is introduced to the marital demands which seem to have left her mother so demolished. It is interesting, incidentally, that Gwendolen does not become pregnant: it is as if a marriage which is partly founded upon the gratification of sado-masochistic compulsions can only end in sterility. And if one considers the class meaning of this match, the social advancement of the upper-middle-class girl to the aristocracy, it doesn't say much for Eliot's belief in class fusion as doing anything to invigorate a morally flaccid culture. Apart from Gwendolen's problematic enlightenment and implicit moral betterment, everything is sterile at the end of *Daniel Deronda*; the only fruitfulness lies in Deronda's mission to put an end to the *diaspora*.

With the decline of the Davilow investments, Gwendolen's hopes for a glamorous existence in which she will call the tune also decline. She has fled from Grandcourt when Lydia Glasher makes her uncompromising declaration of a wronged woman's rights, and she returns to England with the distinctly unglamorous possibility of becoming a governess in front of her. Grandcourt languidly represents himself as a manageable lover. Gwendolen is determined to refuse him, but she is caught between her "disgust and indignation" and the thought of release from the Misses Mompert and what he will do for her mother. Her mamma has "managed badly", and Gwendolen succumbs with the conscious and mistaken belief that she will be able to govern Grandcourt more effectively than her mother has managed her two husbands. She sells herself to Grandcourt for the sake not so much of her own energetic, witting and attractive self, but for the sake of her mother's financial security: she undertakes the male function of providing for female dependants.

Grandcourt knows exactly what he is up to, and he brings along two gorgeous horses to put an expensive seal on the engagement: "These beautiful creatures in their fine grooming, sent a thrill of exultation through Gwendolen. They were the symbols of command and luxury, in delightful contrast with the ugliness of poverty and humiliation at which she had been lately looking close" (Ch. 27). But horses in *Daniel Deronda* take on differing symbolic meanings: it depends on who holds the reins.

Gwendolen loves to ride; she can't wait to "lose" herself in a gallop when she finally accepts Grandcourt and his horses, but Eliot also imagines Gwendolen as the one who is subject to the discipline of the bridle. As she stands with her mother and sisters when they first arrive in Offendene, the image is positive, and Eliot says Gwendolen is like "a young racehorse in the paddock among untrimmed ponies and patient hacks" (Ch. 3). Her gauche sisters are the pony foil for her thoroughbred good looks, and her mother is the patient hack who has been broken and exhausted by familial demands. Gwendolen imagines that

Grandcourt will be as "flawless" a husband as one can manage to secure, that he will allow her to "mount the chariot and drive the plunging horses herself". But Grandcourt is an experienced driver and rider, and he is not about to relinquish the actual and metaphorical reins. When Gwendolen marries him, "in spite of everything" (that is to say, with full knowledge of Lydia Glasher's claims upon him), he feels that she has been "brought to kneel down like a horse under training for the arena" (Ch. 29).

—Deirdre David, Fictions of Resolution in Three Victorian Novels: *North and South, Our Mutual Friend, Daniel Deronda*, (New York: Columbia University Press, 1981): 191–195.

WORKS BY

George Eliot

Translation of David Friedrich Strauss's *The Life of Jesus*
(*Das Leben Jesu*), 1846.
Translation of Ludwig Feuerbach's *The Essence of Christianity*,
1854.
Scenes of Clerical Life, 1858.
Adam Bede, 1859.
"The Lifted Veil," 1859.
The Mill on the Floss, 1860.
"Brother Jacob," 1860.
Silas Marner, 1861.
Romola, 1862.
Felix Holt, the Radical, 1866.
The Spanish Gypsy, 1868.
Middlemarch, 1872.
The Legend of Jubal and Other Poems, 1874.
Daniel Deronda, 1876.
Impressions of Theophrastus Such, 1879.

George Eliot

Adam, Ian, ed. *This Particular Web: Essays on "Middlemarch."* Toronto: University of Toronto Press, 1975.

Allen, Walter. *George Eliot.* New York: Macmillan Co., 1964.

Auerbach, Nina. "Artists and Mothers: A False Alliance." *Women and Literature* 1, vol. 6 (1978): 3–15

Bennett, Joan. *George Eliot: Her Mind and Her Art.* Cambridge: Cambridge University Press, 1948.

Bethell, S.L. "The Novels of George Eliot." *The Criterion*, 18 (1938): 39–57.

Bloom, Harold, ed. *George Eliot.* New Haven: Chelsea House, 1986.

Buckley, Jerome H. ed. *The Worlds of Victorian Fiction.* Cambridge, Mass.: Harvard University Press, 1975.

Carroll, David, ed. *George Eliot, The Critical Heritage.* New York: Barnes & Noble, 1971.

Chase, Cynthia. "The Decomposition of the Elephants: Double-Reading Daniel Deronda." *PMLA 93* (1978): 215–27.

Creeger, George R., ed. *George Eliot: A Collection of Critical Essays.* Englewood Cliffs, N.J.: Prentice-Hall, 1970.

Emery, Laura Comer. *George Eliot's Creative Conflict: The Other Side of Silence.* Berkeley and Los Angeles: University of California Press, 1976.

Ermarth, Elizabeth. "Maggie Tulliver's Long Suicide." *Studies in English Literature* 14 (1974): 587–601.

Garrett, Peter K. *The Victorian Multiplot Novel: Studies in Dialogical Form.* New Haven: Yale University Press, 1980.

Hagan, John. "A Reinterpretation of The Mill on the Floss." *PMLA* 87 (1972): 53–63.

Haight, Gordon S., ed. *A Century of George Eliot Criticism.* London: Methuen, 1966.

Haight, Gordon S., *George Eliot: A Biography*. New York: Oxford University Press, 1968.

Hardy, Barbara. *The Novels of George Eliot: A Study in Form*. New York: Oxford University Press, 1967.

Holmstrom, John, ed. *George Eliot and Her Readers: A Selection of Contemporary Reviews*. New York: Barnes & Noble, 1966.

Karl, Frederick R. *George Eliot: Voice of a Century*. New York: W.W. Norton & Company, 1995.

Kenyon, Frank Wlison. The *Consuming Flame: The Story of George Eliot*. New York: Dodd, Mead, 1970.

Harvey, W.J. *The Art of George Eliot*. New York: Oxford University Press, 1962.

King, Jeanette. *Tragedy in the Victorian Novel: Theory and Practice in the Novels of George Eliot, Thomas Hardy, and Henry James*. Cambridge: Cambridge University Press, 1978.

Leavis, F.R. *The Great Tradition*. London: Chatto & Windus, 1948.

Liddell, Robert. *The Novels of George Eliot*. New York: St. Martin's Press, 1977.

Mann, Karen B. *The Language that Makes George Eliot's Fiction*. Baltimore: The Johns Hopkins University Press, 1983.

McGowan, John P. "The Turn of George Eliot's Realism." *Nineteenth-Century Fiction* 35 (1980): 171-92.

Mintz, Alan L. *George Eliot and the Novel of Vocation*. Cambridge: Harvard University Press, 1978.

Newton, K.M. *George Eliot: Romantic Humanist*. Totowa, N.J.: Barnes & Noble, 1981.

Pinion, F.B. *A George Eliot Companion: Literary Achievement and Modern Significance*. Totawa, N.J.: Barnes & Noble, 1981.

Pritchett, V.S. *The Living Novel*. New York: Reynal & Hitchcock, 1947.

Proust, Marcel. *Marcel Proust on Art and Literature*. London: Chatto and Windus, 1957.

Redinger, Ruby V. *George Eliot: The Emergent Self*. New York: Knopf, 1975.

Smith, Anne, ed. *George Eliot: Centenary Essays and an Unpublished Fragment*. Totowa, N.J.: Barnes & Noble, 1980.

Stephen, Leslie. *George Eliot*. New York: AMS, 1973.

Stone, Donald D. *The Romantic Impulse in Victorian Fiction*. Cambridge: Harvard University Press, 1980.

Stump, Reva. *Movement and Vision in George Eliot's Novels*. Seattle: University of Washington Press, 1959.

Thale, Jerome. *The Novels of George Eliot*. New York: Columbia University Press, 1959.

Wiley, Basil. *Nineteenth Century Studies*. London: Chatto and Windus, 1949.

ACKNOWLEDGMENTS

"George Eliot" by Virginia Woolf. *Discussions of George Eliot*, ed. Richard Stang, (Boston: D.C. Heath and Company, 1960): 28–30. © 1960 by D.C. Heath and Company. Reprinted by permission of Houghton Mifflin.

George Eliot by Gillian Beer (Bloomington: Indiana University Press, 1986): 87–93. © 1986 by Indiana University Press. Reprinted by permission.

Showalter, Elaine; *A Literature of Their Own: British Women Novelists from Bronte to Lessing.* Copyright © 1977 by Princeton University Press. Reprinted by permission of Princeton University Press.

Reading Women, Essays in Feminist Criticism by Mary Jacobus, (Columbia University Press, 1986): 69–72. Copyright © 1986 by Mary Jacobus. All rights reserved. Reprinted by permission.

"Criticisms and Interpretations" by W.D. Howells. From *The Mill on the Floss* by George Eliot, Vol. IX. *Harvard Classics Shelf of Fiction* (New York: P.F. Collier & Son, 1917; Bartleby.com, 2000). Reprinted by permission.

"Vision and Design" by Joan Bennett. From *Discussions of George Eliot*, ed. Richard Stang, (Boston: D.C. Heath and Company, 1960): 64–65. © 1960 by D.C. Heath and Company. Reprinted by permission of Houghton Mifflin.

George Eliot and Community: A Study in Social Theory and Fictional Form by Suzanne Graver (Berkeley: University of California Press, 1984): 194–197. © 1984 by Suzanne Graver. Reprinted by permission.

George Eliot's Early Novels: The Limits of Realism by U.C. Knoepflmacher (Berkeley: University of California Press, 1968): 194–198. © 1968 by the University of California Press. Reprinted by permission.

"George Eliot's Fable for Her Times: *Silas Marner*" by Jerome Thale. From *Discussions of George Eliot*, ed. Richard Stang, (Boston: D.C. Heath and Company, 1960): 97–99. © 1960 by

The Madwoman in the Attic: The Woman Writer and the Nineteenth-Century Imagination by Sandra M. Gilbert and Susan Gubar (New Haven: Yale University Press, 1979): 510–512; 514–516. © 1979 by Yale University Press. Reprinted by permission of Yale University Press.

"George Eliot: The Wisdom of Balancing Claims" by D.A. Miller. From *George Eliot*, ed. K.M. Newton, (New York: Longman Group, 1991): 193–197. © 1991 by The Longman Group. Reprinted by permission.

"Irony in the Mind's Life; Maturity: George Eliot's Middlemarch" by Robert Coles. From *The Critical Response to George Eliot*, ed. Karen L. Pangallo, (Westport, Connecticut: Greenwood Press, 1994): 179–185. © 1994 by Greenwood Press. Reprinted by permission of Greenwood Press.

"The Moral Imagination of George Eliot" by Bert G. Hornback. From *The Critical Response to George Eliot*, ed. Karen L. Pangallo, (Westport, Connecticut: Greenwood Press, 1994): 165–167. © 1994 by Greenwood Press. Reprinted by permission of Greenwood Press.

The Realistic Imagination: English Fiction from Frankenstein to Lady Chatterly by George Levine (Chicago: The University of Chicago Press, 1981): 264–269. © 1981 by The University of Chicago Press. Reprinted by permission.

"Imagery in George Eliot's Last Novels" by Barbara Hardy. From *Discussions of George Eliot*, ed. Richard Stang, (Boston: D.C. Heath and Company, 1960): 82–84. © 1960 by D.C. Heath and Company. Reprinted by permission.

Forms of Life: Character and Moral Imagination in the Novel by Martin Price (New Haven: Yale University Press, 1983): 164–165. © 1983 by Yale University Press. Reprinted by permission of Yale University Press.

From *George Eliot and the Landscape of Time: Narrative Form and Protestant Apocalyptic History* by Mary Wilson Carpenter. Copyright © 1986 by the University of North Carolina Press. Used by permission of the publisher.

Themes of Ideas

MIDDLEMARCH, 77–125; Arthur Brooke in, 77–80, 82–84, 114; Celia Brooke in, 77–78, 83–84, 103, 107–108, 119; Dorothea Brooke in, 15, 77–85, 87–90, 96–108, 114–120, 122–123, 143, 146–147; Harriet Bulstrode in, 82–83, 86, 104; Nicholas Bulstrode in, 77–83, 85, 95, 104, 106–113, as a complex character, 106–113; Elinor Cadwaller in, 81, 84, 96, 98, 119; Edward Casaubon in, 77–80, 83–85, 88, 96–100, 106, 108, 114, 123; characters in, 83–86; characterization in, 93–95; Sir James Chettam in, 77–79, 83–84, 107–108; critical views on, 15, 87–125, 133, 142, 146; Mr. Dagley in, 79, 84; Camden Farebrother in, 79–80, 82, 84, 91–93, 119; Peter Featherstone in, 77–78, 84–86; Caleb Garth in, 78–82, 84–86, 108; Mary Garth in, 77–78, 80, 82, 84–86; images of entrapment in, 96–100; Will Ladislaw in, 77–86, 88, 99, 101, 106, 114–117, 120; Tertius Lydgate in, 15, 77–86, 91–95, 98–100, 106–108, 114,116, 119–120, 124–125; narration and "the classic realist text" in, 90–93; Naumann in, 78, 85, 115–116; perspective from Dorothea's point of view in, 100–106; plot summary of, 77–82; questions of unreliability in, 118–125; John Raffles in, 79–83, 85, 94–95, 109–113; realism in, 114–118; Joshua Rigg in, 79, 83–85; role of Saint Theresa in, 87–90; Walter Tyke in, 78, 85–86; Fred Vincy in, 77–80, 82, 84–86; Lucy Vincy, 84, 86; Rosamond Vincy in, 77, 79–82, 85–86, 93, 96, 99–101, 103–104, 120, 124; Walter Vincy in, 82–83, 86; Mr. Wench in, 78, 86

MILL ON THE FLOSS, THE, 16–46; characters in, 20–21; clash of present and future in, 43–46; critical views on, 14, 22–46, 54, 133; Lucy Deane in, 17–21, 25, 30, 36, 41; Mr. Deane, 21, 44–46; Mrs. Deane in, 21; demands of complex heroines in, 22–24; feminine passion and male repression in, 29–32; Mr. Glegg in, 16–17, 21, 28; Mrs. Glegg in, 17, 21, 28, 38; Stephen Guest in, 18–21, 23, 30–31, 36, 38–39, 41–42, 45; heavy-handed ending of, 36–37; Bob Jakin in, 17–18; Dr. Kenn in, 18–19, 21; maxims and the language that undoes them in, 32–35; Luke Moggs in, 21, Mr. Moss in, 17, 20–21; Mrs. Moss in, 16–18, 21, 38; passion as intellectual need in, 24–29; plot summary of 16–19; principles of tragedy in, 39–43; Mr. Pullett in, 21; Mrs. Pullett in, 17, 21, 38; Reverend Walter Stelling in, 16, 21, 26, 28, 32–33, 35, 44; Edward Tulliver in, 16–18, 20–21, 38, 43–45; Elizabeth Tulliver in, 16–17, 20, 38; Maggie Tulliver in, 16–44, 56, 96–98; Maggie's adversity in,